Grace in All Th

Grace in
All Things

John B. Coburn

Foreword by M. Thomas Shaw, S.S.J.E.

COWLEY PUBLICATIONS
Cambridge ✦ Boston
Massachusetts

Published in the United States of America by Cowley Publications, a division of the Society of St. John the Evangelist. No portion of this book may be reproduced, stored in or introduced into a retrieval system, or transmitted, in any form or by any means—including photocopying—without the prior written permission of Cowley Publications, except in the case of brief quotations embodied in critical articles and reviews.

Library of Congress Cataloging in Publication Data:
Coburn, John B.
Grace in all things / John B. Coburn: foreword by M. Thomas Shaw.
p.   cm.
ISBN 1-56101-113-4 (alk. paper)
1. Prayer. 2. Grace (Theology) 3. Preaching. I. Title.
BL560.C63 1995   95-10659
251--dc20   CIP

Quotations from *Lectures on Preaching* by Phillips Brooks are taken from the Lyman Beecher Lectureship on Preaching, delivered before the Divinity School of Yale College in January and February, 1877, and published in Volume 2 of the Handy Theological Library (London: H. R. Allenson, 1904).

Scripture quotations are taken from the New Revised Standard Version.

Editor: Cynthia Shattuck
Book designer and typesetter: Vicki Black
Cover design by Vicki Black.

This book is printed on recycled, acid-free paper
and was produced in the United States of America.

Cowley Publications
28 Temple Place
Boston, Massachusetts 02111

To
Douglas V. Steere
*whose friendship and writings have helped me
realize that "it is for God alone my soul
in silence waits"*

Theodore O. Wedel
*who introduced me to the theology of
Frederick Denison Maurice, and whose preaching
and teaching embodied both its glorious freedom
and challenging mystery*

and
Alan Whittemore, O.H.C.
*who said, "If what you want to do you can do
for God's sake, do it; if you can't, don't."*

Contents

Acknowledgments

I wish to acknowledge my indebtedness to:

The Reverend Sheryl Kujawa
*who rummaged through some of my papers
and helped select these;*

Cynthia Shattuck,
*whose editorial hand sharpened both
my language and ideas;*

and
My wife, Ruth,
*who lived whatever wisdom about grace is written here
long before I either thought of it or expressed it.*

Foreword

M. Thomas Shaw, S.S.J.E.,
Bishop of Massachusetts

I do not see John Coburn as often as I did when he was the Bishop of Massachusetts and I was the Superior of the Society of St. John the Evangelist. John is eighty years old now and lives some distance from Boston, and I am a too-busy bishop at the beginning of a new ministry. I miss him. I miss our telephone conversations and I miss the hours of talk in his living room.

So I am grateful for the opportunity to read this book because it places me in the presence of John Coburn. His wisdom, his humanity, his care for people, his joy, and his prayer are all here in these pages. In this short book we find the essence of his long life as a pastor, husband, father, leader, teacher, preacher, friend, and, most of all, a man of prayer.

This book is different from other books I have reviewed or for which I have written forewords because I keep going back to it. In the months since it was first given to me in manuscript form, I have never finished with it. I find myself, in the midst of my new and challenging ministry, picking up these pages in the early morning before I pray and being reminded by John of what is important in ministry and what is essential to the life of faith. I am so new in this ministry, and reading this book has given me something I need: to be accompanied by an older, wiser, more experienced brother in Christ. John's reflections have refreshed my courage, perspective, and one of the most important of all virtues for the contemporary Christian, hope. I pray more honestly after I read this book. I look a little deeper into my life with God. I feel less anxious, more trusting in God. I take myself less seriously than I and others seem to be taking me these days.

Because this book encourages us as we make our way into the kingdom of God, it is classic spiritual reading. The journey into the heart of God is a mysterious one, full of strange turns, the appropriation of tragic events we never dreamed we would be able to appropriate into our lives, dangerous joy, paradox, and perplexity. It is a journey too hard, too odd, and too long to make alone. And so our God, the abundant provider, is always offering us companions along the way to help us on the journey. Companions who make real for us Jesus' words that his yoke is easy and his burden is light. This book, because the author has accepted the companions God has offered to him, is now our companion. Read it slowly, meditatively, reflecting on your own experience. Let it help you own your prayer, and you will find yourself strengthened and supported by a whole community of saints, past and present, of whom John Coburn is one.

In publishing this book, Cowley Publications offers us an invitation not unlike those deceptively simple invitations of Jesus in the Gospel. Jesus is always inviting his disciples to come, to sit and rest, to wait, to follow, to hear, to see. When his disciples have the courage to accept his invitation they find themselves somewhere at a banquet in the realm of the kingdom of God. You are a disciple of Jesus Christ, however tentative or uncertain you are about your faith. If you accept the invitation to read this book, you will find yourself taking your rightful place in the kingdom of God. Not because the author is holy, but because like all of the classic spiritual writers he is transparent, through his prayer, to the holiness of God.

Cambridge, Massachusetts
April, 1995

Grace

*Be your own best self for your people's
sake. That is the true law of the minister's
devotion....The minister and the
congregation belong together.*

— Phillips Brooks —

As I began to prepare these reflections, it seemed to me prudent to read again what one of my predecessors as Bishop of Massachusetts said when he delivered the Beecher Lectures at Yale Divinity School in 1877. At that time Phillips Brooks was rector of Trinity Church, Boston, and would not become bishop for another fifteen years. He is remembered today more as preacher than as bishop, more for his sermons than for his episcopal acts. Episcopal acts, after all, do not require as much ability as does preaching—nor as much hard work!

I had last read those lectures when I was a student at Union Seminary some forty-five years ago. All I could recall was Phillips Brooks's principal and most famous point, that preaching essentially conveys "truth through personality." In these lectures Brooks had much good advice to offer the preacher besides, and it ranges from the lyrical—"Every true preacher must be a poet....A belief in the Incarnation in the Divine Son of Man makes poets of us all"—to down-to-earth counsel about pastoral stability:

> First, have as few congregations as you can. Second, know your congregation as thoroughly as you can. Third, know your congregation so largely and deeply that in knowing it you shall know humanity.

Rereading his words now, so many years later, confirms my own conviction, reached after countless sermons preached and listened to, that when all is said and done, it is *who* the preacher is in his or her deepest self that determines the effectiveness of the sermon in the minds and hearts of its hearers.

I am not referring to the charm of the preacher's personality, nor to how it would come out on a psychological test or personality inventory—to what degree introvert or extrovert, normal or neurotic. The question instead is this: does the Spirit of God dwell in the spirit of the preacher in such a way that when the sermon is finished, it is God's truth that has been heard? Or is the sermon simply the preacher's opinion about things? In Phillips Brooks's words, "Some preachers are always preaching the last book they have read, and their congregations always find it out."

It is my conviction that *preaching is molded by the person,* that *the person is molded by God,* and that *that relation is shaped through prayer.*

The first question I want to ask is, Is there any difference between prayer for the preacher and prayer for everyone else? The answer is both yes and no. It is no because prayer as a response to God is the same for everyone. We are all invited to trust God, to place our lives in God's hands, to try to discern what God wants us to do with those lives and then to go about living them as best we can. Of course there will be countless distinctions as to how those lives should be led, but fundamentally prayer is the same for everyone. Watch; pay attention to what is going on in your life; be present to God, and see or sense what he is doing; offer yourself in faith to him. Worship God with others; then try to carry out your life loving the neighbors you know personally and working for justice and peace for the sake of the neighbors you don't.

Though the preacher is a baptized member of Christ's church, called to be a Christian just like *every* other Christian, there *is* a special calling for the preacher, and that is to preach God's Word. Preaching God's Word means struggling and praying that the Word preached is, indeed, the Word of God and not simply a series of interesting opinions. The preacher is to become a part of God's Word—to get inside it, belong to it, have it incarnate in his or her being; in a sense, to *become* God's Word. This is the special calling of the preacher.

Early in my days as dean at the Episcopal Theological School, I was returning one Saturday sunny afternoon in the fall from watching a football game in Soldiers' Field in Cambridge (where I usually cheered for Harvard except when they were playing Princeton and—I must confess—especially when they were playing Yale). As I walked by the library, one of the new students came out. I said, "Jack, for heaven's sake, what are you doing studying inside on such a lovely day so early in the year?"

"Oh, Dean," he replied, "I am so happy here doing all this reading with these exciting courses that I can't even remember what it was like to be a lay person!" When I heard this I shuddered: here, in only two months' time, we had already corrupted him, begun to separate him from those whose servant he was called to be.

A preacher's life of prayer *does* have a distinctive quality, but its purpose is to enhance his or her preach-

ing, not to move away from or stand over the congregation. Preachers have the responsibility—just as lay persons do—to keep in touch with themselves as part of
humanity, so they can identify themselves with their people. At the same time, they are not to forget that they are
called to a special vocation: to preach the Gospel. And
for that, prayer is essential. This calling is a special
and—I'll say it outright—a *holy* calling. To be called by
God to the ministry is a wonderful way to spend a life-
time. If it's not a call from God, it's a hell of a way to
earn a living.

So what makes the difference between a preacher's
prayer and everyone else's is that the former has a special assignment to preach. It is God's call. "I have chosen you to be with me," Jesus said to his disciples. That
is us. "I will also send you out to preach and you will
have authority over the demons," he told them. Since
God is the one who calls, our response is to him, and
that response is with our whole life. That is our prayer.
To continue throughout our ministry to retain that sense
of being called by God for the special task of preaching
is, I believe, the most important factor in preaching. It is
nurtured by prayer. Without prayer, the sense of calling
goes.

To receive such a call is a gift from God. It is sheer
grace. However we receive it, we know it is not because
we deserve it. If we have it, it does no good to ask why.
That is a mystery, just as God is. All we do is accept it
and thank God for it. It is a personal experience of grace
and is meant to open our eyes to the grace all around
us, in all times and all places, all events and all people,
everywhere and always.

Prayer for the preacher is the preacher's response to
God through his or her living in the Spirit, for it is the
Spirit who provides the connecting link between the

preacher and the hearers of the sermon. Participation in the Spirit by the one who preaches and the ones who listen means that the Word is both spoken and heard. The Spirit in the preacher searches for the Spirit in the hearers to waken them to heed the Spirit already present in them, and therefore lived.

It is in living in the Spirit that it is possible to preach the Word of God and hear the Word of God. If the Spirit does not live in the preacher, the Word will not be preached, and if the Spirit does not live in the listeners, it will not be heard. It is the Spirit who speaks through the Word, and the one who preaches and the ones who hear are those who live it—or, more compassionately and perhaps more realistically, want to live it. As Robert Bellah said in another context, "Revolutionaries who in their own lives do not embody the future cannot bring it." So it might be said, "Preachers who in their own lives do not in some way embody the Gospel cannot proclaim it, much less bring it." I insert that phrase "in some way" because we need to be very cautious, very tentative, about identifying who has or does not have the Spirit of God, or indeed describing too sharply or positively the Spirit itself.

The Spirit cannot be captured by definition or proposition; it is like the wind which comes and goes of its own volition. We don't know where it comes from, or why, or where it goes. It is like breath. We can breathe—when we do, we are alive, and when we stop we are dead—but we cannot create breath. It is given to us; all we can do is to be open to it and receive it. We can be helped to discern the spirits, but that does not mean we can package them. It is by observing how the lives all around us are lived that we can best discern the Holy Spirit within them. Do we see less arrogance at work in them and more humility, more concern for others?

As for spirit in general, we can, I think, make our own the comment of Gerald May in *Will and Spirit:*

> It seems to me that spirit has something to do with the energy of our lives, the life-force that keeps us active and dynamic....Spirit...has a quality of connecting us with each other, with the world around us, and with the mysterious Source of all. When this idea of Spirit is perceived as energy coming from God, it is called the Holy Spirit.

Now, how can we get at this Spirit and identify it in the preacher? It is not likely, though possible, that we will find it simply by reading his or her sermons. Frederick Denison Maurice, considered by many to be *the* leading Anglican theologian, once wrote:

> The best way to understand a theologian is not to analyze the fine points of his clever controversial works, but rather to enter into the heart of his spiritual meditations, those works in which the theologian is cultivating fellowship with God and most forgetting himself.

Christian literature, from Saint Augustine's *Confessions* to Karl Rahner's *Encounter with Silence,* attests to the truth of this observation. If we can understand how theologians view their personal relationship to God, we get a deeper understanding of their theology than by simply reading their theological works. And the same is true of preachers. The best way to understand them is not to analyze the fine points of their sermons, but rather to enter into those works in which the preacher is cultivating fellowship with God and most deeply revealing his or her relationship to God.

The kind of person the preacher is leaves its mark upon the sermon. We have to beware of the gap we sometimes find between the words of a preacher and who he or she really is: "I couldn't believe what the sermon said because I couldn't believe the preacher. The words and the person don't go together." If the preacher doesn't ring true, then the words themselves have a hollow sound. They have little power to convert us or even to help us come to a better understanding of ourselves.

Often, of course, because of the personality and character of the preacher, the Word of God is heard even though the sermon construction may leave much to be desired. A parishioner once commented about the preaching of his rector: "He doesn't, in fact, give many brilliant sermons, but it doesn't seem to make all that much difference because of the kind of person he is. If all he did was to stand up and say, 'God is love,' we would know it to be true because that is the way he lives—with that kind of spirit. And, therefore, we are fed, week by week." This must be something of what Phillips Brooks meant when he spoke of preaching as the art of communicating "truth through personality" and insisted that "what is in the sermon must be in the preacher first."

Preaching is in many ways a great mystery: there is no formula which guarantees that what a preacher intends to say is what is actually heard. The Spirit in the lives of the people often interprets words differently for different people.

Early in my ministry, for example, I preached what I considered to be a profound sermon on Christian marriage. After the service I had a phone call from a young couple saying they had been greatly helped by what I had to say, and could they come and see me? Could they! They arrived, and after they had sat down, I asked them, quietly preening myself, "And what was it that was so helpful?" They proceeded then to explain to me what they thought were the three points of the sermon (those were the days when every sermon had three points!) in exactly the opposite way from what I had intended. They had listened to the sermon all right, but their interpretation was so far away from what I intended as to be quite bizarre. What they heard was what they were prepared to hear. The Spirit had come to the rescue and given them the meaning they needed for their lives at that moment; their marriage was strengthened and they stayed together.

In preaching, one preaches "in the Spirit" as truly as one can. The words then go and can never be recalled. Sometimes you say words on the spur of the moment you never intended to say. Never mind. The Spirit will pick them up and place them in the hearts and minds of those hearers who listen "in the Spirit," who are trying to be open to what the Word of God may mean. Our words will mean different things to different people who bring different lives and different experiences to the hearing of the Word.

All we can say is, "Those who have ears to hear, hear," and who those hearers are, God alone knows. It is in the hidden "cave of the heart" that the Spirit moves. The preacher can offer the sermon to the hearers, and at the same time offer it to God, and can then forget about it. To have some distance from it, to be free from obsession by success or failure, is to be able to learn from our mistakes and not to be discouraged by them (or to be overly proud of "That was a fine sermon, Pastor"), but to try to move on into a deeper understanding of the text as we prepare and pray over the next sermon. "For we do not proclaim ourselves; we proclaim Jesus Christ as Lord and ourselves as your slaves for Jesus' sake" (2 Corinthians 4:5). This is simply to say that the Christ we know is the Christ we preach. We show forth that Christ as we serve our people, and they know it. Our commitment is to live the Gospel as well as we can, and the rest is up to God.

Some years ago I lived with and reflected on the prologue from Saint John's gospel, particularly this part of it:

> And the Word became flesh and lived among us, and we have seen his glory, the glory as of a father's only son, full of grace and truth....From his fullness we have all received, grace upon grace. (John 1:14, 16)

I was preparing a series of meditations for the annual retreat of a women's religious order, the Sisters of Saint Margaret, at their summer convent in Duxbury near Cape Cod. That particular week—the last week in August—was cold, windy, rainy, and foggy. There were eleven meditations during that retreat, with five homilies thrown in at no extra charge. The sisters sat patiently in their seats in the chapel open to the elements; I sat in my trenchcoat, which by the end of the week was soggy and wet.

On the final morning the sun broke through, the fog lifted—along with our spirits—and at breakfast we burst into conversation after five days of silence. I drove off down the Cape, my heart lightened, relieved (I suppose) because the retreat was over and if the meditations and homilies had not been brilliant (though helped by Raymond Brown and the Anchor Bible), I had at least given it all I could.

On Route 28 near Hyannis it suddenly dawned on me that I was hungry. Religious communities, especially when on retreat, serve meals which, while nutritious and full of vitamins, do not, as they used to say, "stick to the stomach." I noticed a Dunkin' Donuts by the side of the road, turned into the parking lot, purchased a cup of coffee and a sugar doughnut, and went back to my car. I leaned against the hood, basking in the warm sun (and in some measure of self-righteousness), when a truck drove up on the side of the road and stopped. The truck driver leaned out the window and shouted, "How's the doughnut, Father?" I shouted back, "Excellent!" "Good!" he said, and drove off.

I was dumbstruck, delighted, almost ecstatic. What a surprise! What a fellow! What a sense of humor! I was simply overcome and made one with everything—all existence—at that moment. I was one with the driver, one with his humor, one with the coffee and doughnut, one with life, one even with God. In fact, the thought went through my mind that God himself had planned that ecstasy. Needless to say, when I returned home that afternoon to my wife and family, I was a good deal more human, more fun to be with than when I had left, weighted down (so I thought) with all the responsibilities I was carrying.

As I reflected upon that event (and you may have sensed that I reflected upon it a lot), it seemed to me that it was, in fact, grace. It wasn't a symbol of grace nor an illustration of grace nor a parable of grace, but grace itself.

It came, in the first instance, just out of the blue. Nobody planned it. Nobody prepared for it. It just came, a sheer gift. It encompassed me, enveloped me, made me a part of everything that was going on: the sun and its warmth; the truck driver and his humor; the coffee and the doughnut. We all belonged together. I even belonged to and was one with myself—and so with all of existence, of life, of God. Everything was a unity, all the pieces fitted. Perfect harmony. All was complete and whole.

To be sure it was a momentary event. It couldn't last forever. Life moves on. Perhaps the driver drove on, had a beer for lunch, two beers, too many beers, speeded, drove over a child. The perfection, the wholeness may have been smashed to pieces. Yet the memory of the event itself is recalled to my mind as real, substantial, eternal.

Two other characteristics of grace can be identified in this event. The first is that grace is a gift; it comes undeserved—one does not earn it and cannot work for it. One can only accept it. And as in other relationships when one receives a gift, one can only say "thank you." The question, of course, is who do you say "thank you" to and what do you say "thank you" for? The second characteristic is that when one is graced in this way, one goes on a more whole human being, easier to live with, more loving, more willing not to be in control, not to insist on having one's way, more tolerant of others' foibles, more willing to let be, more trusting of the whole process of living, more affirming, caring, and supporting—at least, so it seems to me.

Now what, you may ask, does this have to do with prayer and preaching? Well, that depends. It depends upon you and your experiences, whether you have ever had any similar experiences, and on what you make of them. It depends on what you think they mean and what, if anything, you do—or have done, or will do—about them. How you respond is your prayer. Prayer is response to life. Everybody responds in one way or another. A Christian's response is to God, faith and trust in God as the creating Word without whom nothing was made that was made.

There is, of course, no guarantee that God is responsible, that the whole experience of Christian living is not simply a fantasy. Faith is a gamble. It is risky, and it may not even be true. As Thomas Merton wrote to a friend in 1962: "The law of all spiritual life is the law of risk and struggle, and of possible failure." Toward the end of his life Merton also quoted the *Spiritual Canticle* of Saint John of the Cross in his writings on contemplative prayer. If you want to find God (and this seems to me to be the heart of the matter), then

> seek him in faith and love...for these two are the guides of the blind which will lead thee, by a way thou knowest not, to the hidden place of God. Because faith...is like the feet where with the soul journeys to God, and love is the guide that directs it.

How we respond to such experiences is our prayer. It is not, therefore, so much what one says—although "saying one's prayers" is not to be neglected—as it is how one responds to life, both its events filled with grace and its events filled with evil, its moments that inspire and its moments that bring despair. With what spirit and in what style we respond to life reflects our true life of prayer.

To respond in the Spirit of Christ is to respond through the Word, and this is to preach the Word. So prayer for the preacher is his or her response to the experiences of living in that Spirit. Another way of putting it is to say that the preacher prepares for preaching by being transformed by the Spirit of Christ, so that the response is *from* God *to* God, one with God and with those who are members of Christ's body. This is "being one in the Spirit."

Grace is everywhere. We don't own it and we cannot control it; we can only see it, receive it, and respond to it. That means to act gracefully ourselves, and the best way to do that is to thank the "author of grace" for all those who bear it, live it, and give it. And to try to go and do likewise. That is prayer.

A book by Ronald Blythe called *Divine Landscapes* was published in England a number of years ago. In this book Blythe considered the relationship of landscapes to literature, including religious literature. He wrote:

> Britain's natural contours are drawn all over the religious symbols and references, most of them Christian though many of earlier faiths. There is scarcely a field or a hill, let alone a village or a town, which cannot be read in

both spiritual and material terms. Buildings and plants, weather and views, creatures and stones, seasons and roads, rivers and soils, gardens and forests, skies and caves, all that is, as Julian of Norwich put it, are doubly immersed in a sacred tradition and in a science.

I dwell upon this close relationship, this identity, between the world of nature and human nature for two reasons: first, because from the dawn of history it has been one of the sources of strength for the human enterprise. The known has pressed in upon us to help us face the unknown, to give us courage, to lift our vision, and to give us openings for grace, hope. The natural landscape of hills, valleys, canyons, caves, mountains, and deserts has helped shape the spirit of our ancestors.

Natural contours often have become religious symbols, or have reflected them, and have helped penetrate the mystery of creation by the divine. Since the Word who created us was made flesh and dwelt among us, we are helped by faith to see him in all his works. "The earth is the Lord's and all that therein is," and the Incarnation means our identification with, not mastery of, much less exploitation of, nature. We belong, as Julian of Norwich put it, to "all that is."

The second reason is that, from childhood, I have sensed a mysterious "other world" in nature: in sunsets and sunrises, in rippling water and flowing brooks, in special trees or groves of trees, in waves crashing, wind rustling, grasses waving, birds flying, thunder clapping, rain falling. With part of my nature I have always been a little suspicious of this tendency in myself: too sentimental perhaps, not sound theologically.

Then one day in a class at Union Seminary I heard Paul Tillich describe how he came to discover the meaning of what he called "treedom," and I found myself understanding what he was saying—which I didn't always!

He described how in the woods in Germany he once sat down at the base of a tree, leaned against the trunk, and pondered the mystery of what it meant to be a tree:

> I pressed against the bark, pressed through it, let the roots carry me sinking into the ground, was carried upward through the branches to the leaves fluttering as the breezes passed through. I felt that I had become one with that tree, and was welcomed into the mystery of treedom.

There was at least a streak of nature-mysticism in Tillich. He is reported to have said of his colleague Reinhold Niebuhr, "Poor Reinie, he can never see God in a sunset because he keeps looking for him in the Scriptures." The fact is, God can be seen in both the Scriptures and sunsets, even sunsets that are polluted by the factories of Jersey City, Hoboken, and Secaucus.

To be in Christ means that we can open our eyes to see by faith and imagination his Spirit in the world of nature. To see, in Wordsworth's phrase,

> a presence that disturbs me
>   with the joy of elevated thoughts,
> a sense sublime of something far more deeply interfused
>   of a central peace subsisting at the heart
>   of endless agitation.

I am now convinced that the sunsets I saw each evening when I was in the Pacific during the war held me together because God was in them, not just because they were inspiring in themselves.

None of this is to deny that nature, as well as human nature, is fallen, that earthquakes, floods, fires, and tornadoes destroy and devastate. Nor is it to deny that the devil as well as God may speak through nature. As Luther warned, "The devils are in woods, in waters, in wildernesses, and in dark, pooly places, ready to hurt and prejudice people."

The significance of our affirming our relation to and identification with nature is that it may also lead to affirming our relation with Christ and to union with him. It may be that a rediscovery of the identification of God with his creation through his Son as creator and through his Spirit as sustainer may bring with it a confidence, a zest, and a joy often lacking in many religious practices. The life of the Spirit is an energized life as we are possessed by an intimate relationship with the divine.

If we can come to an understanding and sense of "treedom" by pressing close to a tree, surely we can come to a deeper, more personal understanding of Christ by pressing close to him—or, more accurately, by opening ourselves to him so he may press more closely to us, that we may become like him. The goal of our prayer and our preaching is that we and those who share with us in worship may be transformed into Christ through union with him.

There are, then, I believe, *places* of grace. And there are *people* of grace—that is, people who by their spirit affirm us. We may know them, or we may only have heard of them or read about them. Some of these people of grace may recognize themselves as such, but most of them probably do not. They may have religious convictions or they may not. I have no idea of the religious convictions—of lack thereof—of the truck driver who greeted me, but he certainly showered grace on me.

Whatever else they are, people of grace are fully *themselves*: the outstanding characteristic they have in common is that they are *whole*. Such people seem to have a natural humility. There is an unself-consciousness about them. They are usually surprised when told they have brought grace to anyone. They do not puff themselves up, do not make demands upon others; they just present themselves as they are—and in that authentic presentation they strengthen and affirm others.

People of grace are not embarrassed by who they are or what their gifts may be, but they don't take themselves too seriously, either. They sit rather lightly to life, taking it as it comes, engaging in it as their convictions prompt them. They tend to be "inner" directed rather that "outer"—that is, they act not to make an impression, but because they have certain convictions about what is right. They act according to what counts most for the betterment of society and for the care of their friends, colleagues, and whoever else comes into their lives.

Even though they would probably never claim to possess grace, much less know God, such people possess the characteristics of grace. Grace is God's outgoing love for us. It comes out of his inner nature and is simply who he is. When that nature is expressed and we experience it, we know that we are loved just as we are and we are strengthened. Life takes on a different color: more light, less darkness; more joy, less despair; more jokes at our expense, less at others; more foolishness, less solemnity; more somersaults and kicking up of our heels, less dragging our feet and sighs of self-pity.

There was a time when I would have identified only those who loved me and whom I loved as grace-bearers. They were the ones with whom I felt most "at one." Our mutual trust, our mutual giving and concern, caring and compassion, were, I thought, intimations of God's out-going love for us. In union—of mind, of body, of spirit—with another, we were in some mysterious way in union also with God. We were filled by God, uplifted by God, and we knew we belonged to God. We suspected (or hoped) that these feelings were intimations of our true home with him. God's Spirit was touching our spirits through human trust and love, so our dealings were not only with the ones we loved but also with God himself.

Then, gradually, the company of people in whom I saw (and sometimes felt) compassion and caring grew. It was not simply that they cared, but that they were ex-pressing (whether they knew it or not) a compassionate and caring spirit from beyond themselves. That seemed to me to be God's Spirit at work. In my experience, there was no other reason that would cause certain peo-ple to give of themselves so generously, in ways that sometimes consumed them, and in what could only be termed forms of self-sacrifice.

Finally I came to perceive that even those who would put me down, who were set against me (wanted my job, wished me to fail, or whatever) in some curious way were also revealing something of God's Spirit to me. God wanted me to see him in those flawed relationships as well as in the "comfortable" ones. I came to see, for example, that the arrogance I detected in someone set against me existed in some measure in me as well: "Who does he think he is?" Well, who do I think I am? In an in-creasing number of relationships I considered broken or antagonistic, it was clear that someone or something was trying to reveal some truth about my own nature.

What was that Spirit? Who was that Spirit? My dear friend, the late Cardinal Archbishop of Boston, Hum-berto Medeiros, used to say, "Jesus comes into my office every day in each person who comes to see me. Some-

times he comes in deep disguise." We can usually un-
mask him if we wait and do not panic or hit back, if we
pray for the discerning eye of faith and then look at ourselves again. One of the keys to pastoral counseling, in
my experience, is to listen—or try to listen—to what the
Spirit is saying to me. Then, perhaps, I will have something helpful, caring, and loving to say to the person.

All of this is simply to say that God's love comes
through every kind of human relationship. That is what
the Incarnation means: God's creation (including all
kinds of people) is permeated with grace. Keep your eye
open to see it. Watch. Pay attention. Then pray and respond.

Well, you will ask, does this also apply to erotic love,
and to love relationships outside and beyond marriage?
Love, in my judgment, enriches life as nothing else can
except, perhaps, the creation of beauty, but that does
not mean that love is always meant to be expressed in
acts of love. Indeed, love is sometimes best expressed
when it is _not_ acted out. One has to choose among
loves.

To say "no" to one love for the sake of another enriches the quality of love. To say "no" to some human
loves in order to respond more fully to divine love is for
some the richest love of all. To refrain from acting out
love in human relationships makes it possible to say,
"Mary—John—I love you best in God." That is _really_
love, for it is God loving you and Mary or John simply
with your cooperation! Chastity may, therefore, be the
most appropriate form of love under those circum-
stances; it is God's love and how we respond to it—not
chastity by itself—that is most important.

The purpose of prayers for all the different kinds of people in our lives is not to give God information about them. The reason for these prayers is twofold. First, it is to commend them to *God* and to make certain we do not simply want to commend them to *ourselves,* as though we owned them or could control them, or even know what is best for them. We can, in fact, "give them up" best by giving them to God. Those we love most are those we separate from ourselves. We need distance from—not attachment to—our loved ones. We can disengage ourselves best by engaging them to God. That is intercessory prayer at its best: that God's will may be done in them.

Second, it is to help us begin to see that even evil is under God; indeed, it may be a part of his created order. The divine includes the demonic; creation includes destruction. In and through all the evil in the world there is also God's redemptive power at work. How this mystery is best understood—although still only partially—is to look at the redemptive power of God's love dying on the cross as Jesus Christ dies. The mystery of evil may not be fully understood, but the cross helps make it bearable.

One of the books that meant so much to seminarians preparing for ministry a generation ago was George Bernanos's *The Diary of a Country Priest.* It is the story of a young priest carrying on his ministry in a difficult country parish with its full share of conflicts, betrayals, sins, failures, victories, and virtues—the stuff of life. In summing up his difficulties (his sense of failing his people and his Lord at the end) and in taking everything into consideration (his people's failures and sins as well as his own) the country priest concludes his diary with, "Grace is everywhere." Since the Word was made flesh and redeemed the *whole* world, grace is everywhere.

Grace is everywhere and it is prayer that enables the preacher to see it. To see it everywhere. If preachers can be "graced" by the experiences of their own lives, then they can preach with grace. Otherwise, they will simply be delivering lectures.

We have received, and continue to receive, grace upon grace in and through all the experiences of life, in and through everything. The reason for this is that the Word became flesh and dwells in every human experience. The Word dwelt among us, full of grace and truth. We have beheld his glory, glory as of the only Son from the Father. From his fullness have we all received, grace upon grace.

Prayer

*A belief in the Incarnation,
in the divine Son of Man,
makes poets of us all.*

— Phillips Brooks —

My first chapter had to do with grace as gifts from God and gifts of God. There are places of grace and persons of grace and events that are full of grace. As we mature in the Christian life we hope we will be helped to discern grace in hitherto unexpected places and persons and events, including, finally, everything and everywhere. The underlying theology is that since Christ has redeemed the world, that world—however fallen—is now an arena, or kingdom, of grace.

This talk has to do with *prayer*. The purpose of prayer is to enable us to see more clearly the evidences of grace in our lives, in our society. The danger is that we are tempted to believe that if we pray better or harder or in some new way, we shall be able to appropriate more grace; in the words of the familiar prayer, we pray that "we may grow in grace as we grow in age." It is a perfectly good prayer so long as we don't think grace comes as a result of our efforts and belongs to us. We, rather, belong to grace: it is a gift; it appropriates us.

Prayer may be thought of as our effort simply to be open to grace. God is everywhere present to us; prayer is our being present to God. It helps us open our eyes of faith to see God, who is a hidden God, more clearly.

A few years ago I had the privilege of teaching a course on contemporary spirituality at Virginia Theological Seminary. I was asked one day if I intended to attend a meeting for the community on the subject of inclusive language, which was (and still is) engaging the energy of many people in the church. "No," I said. "That particular issue is not on the top of my list of priorities." One of the students asked, "Well, what is at the top?"

"The preparation of men and women for the ministry of Christ's church," I replied. "I am really interested in, What kind of people are they? What makes them tick? How did they get to be who they are? How are they going to help the church count for something in our society? Those are the issues that have always seemed most important to me. They have to do with values. Are there any transcendent values above the values that arise out of community? What does the incarnation of those values in Jesus Christ mean? Who is the custodian of those values? What relationship, if any, do they have to the values of the institutional church? So those are my priorities. Any other questions?"

There was a pause. Then a young man said, "Can I ask you a personal question?" I wasn't quite sure what he meant by that, or whether he wanted to ask if there some interesting scandal in my background, but I took a chance and replied, "Certainly, anything under the sun."

"What is the single most important thing a minister should bring to the ministry and how does he or she get it?" he asked.

"All any of us can bring is ourselves and our spirit," I answered. "In the long run I believe that we come to our best selves with the help of some kind of prayer. By prayer I mean simply how we respond to God. It is as much how we live—with what kind of spirit—as it is what we say. If we are open to God and never assume we have captured him or fully understand him, but try to welcome God's Spirit to mix it up with our spirit, and be

willing to wait so that some kind of transformation
through Christ's Spirit may take place—then I think we
have the fundamental ingredients for ministry. Any more
questions?" There were none.

In the course to which I have just referred, we began
each class session with this prayer:

> O God of peace, who has taught us that in returning and
> rest we shall be saved, in quietness and in confidence
> shall be our strength: By the might of your Spirit lift us,
> we pray you, to your presence, where we may be still
> and know that you are God.

Then followed ten minutes of silence. Somewhat to my
surprise when I asked the classes at the end of the se-
mester to fill out the "post-mortem reports" evaluating
the course, one of the favorable things constantly men-
tioned was the ten minutes of silence. (I had assumed, of
course, that my words of wisdom would be considered
the high point!)

If they had learned nothing else, these students had
learned that they could, in fact, sit quietly for ten minutes doing nothing. "All the troubles of life come upon
us," Pascal wrote, "because we refuse to sit quietly for
awhile in our rooms." Sitting is a form of Buddhist meditation. If the students had learned how to be silent and if
they had learned how to breathe properly, they had perhaps learned all a teacher could teach about prayer.
Prayer is not a product you can wrap up and give to
somebody else. It is like "spirit"—elusive, hard to pin
down, hard to teach.

In his book *Prayer and Modern Man,* Jacques Ellul wrote in this connection:

> Prayer is in no sense a thing capable of a perceptible or observable reality. There never can be anything except people who pray. That is the sole reality....When a person does not pray, all the discourse about prayer has no meaning for him.

So when a teacher is asked how to pray, all he or she can say is—pray! Pray as you can, not as you think you should. And although you *can* pray running, jumping, or swimming, cultivating solitude—being quiet, silent, waiting, doing nothing—probably remains the most effective, even indispensable, way of preparing for prayer (as with preparing a sermon).

This is one reason why what is called "centering prayer" is currently so popular. When we settle down, center down, and wait, meaning is often found simply in the waiting, as the Welsh priest and poet R. S. Thomas wrote:

> Moments of great calm
> Kneeling before an altar
>   of wood in a stone church
> In summer, waiting for the God
> To speak, the air a staircase
>   for silence....Prompt me, God,
> But not yet! When I speak,
> Though it be you who speak
>   through me, something is lost.
> The meaning is in the waiting.

Beginning with silence and waiting, we prepare to enter what Kathleen Healy called "the cave of the heart." We are going within to cultivate an attitude in which we keep our heart "in a praying frame," to use the words of the seventeenth-century Puritan minister, John Cotton. It is to help us begin to understand what it means to "pray without ceasing."

Such prayer does not mean repeating words, though a method like the Jesus Prayer, which simply repeats the name of Jesus slowly and rhythmically, may be at certain times a helpful devotional exercise. Prayer means, rather, a disposition to regard life with a sense of wonder and mystery. In *The Sigh,* Abraham Heschel described prayer as the way "to take notice of the wonder, to regain a sense of the mystery that animates all beings, the divine margin in all attainment." To do this takes time and it takes silence; it takes patience and a willingness to do nothing.

The first lesson in learning how to pray, then, is to practice doing nothing. It is to be silent, aware of oneself, aware of God, willing to present oneself to him. It means not to strain, not to control, not to do anything. If distracting thoughts come, let them come; they will go away. If a sense of grace comes, let it come; that too will pass. The point is simply to be—to be in the presence of God.

We are, of course, talking about two great mysteries: the mystery of God and the mystery of ourselves. We have trouble understanding ourselves, to say nothing of trying to understand another human being or trying to understand God. As Karl Rahner asked,

> Who knows the heart of another man? You alone are the reader of hearts, O God, and how can I expect to understand the heart of another when I don't even understand my own?

Our knowledge of God comes from faith: the commitment of ourselves to the mystery of God. Faith is an act of prayer. Bernard Haring wrote:

> Faith lives on prayer; indeed faith is, strictly speaking, nothing other than prayer. From the moment we begin truly to believe we are already praying, and when prayer ends, faith ends also.

Faith does not, in this sense, mean the acceptance of a certain set of beliefs. It is, rather, a giving over of ourselves to the mystery of God. It is "the assurance of things hoped for, the conviction of things not seen" (Hebrews 11:1).

Saint John of the Cross stated that we are to seek God in "faith and love," while the fourteenth-century author of *The Cloud of Unknowing* wrote, "By love may God be gotten and holden, but by thought never." Echoing this in our own century, Edith Stein, a Carmelite nun, philosopher, and contemplative who died in Auschwitz, could write:

> God is not a God of knowledge but God is love. He does not reveal his mysteries to the deductive intelligence but to the heart that surrenders itself to him.

Often our failure to trust God stems from our failure to love him whom we do not see or our brothers and sisters whom we do.

In any case, silence, the mystery of God and the mystery of ourselves, faith and love (and its extension, justice) all belong together. These are the ingredients that go into prayer. They also help to make up the second lesson in prayer: attention to and acceptance of the mystery of God and of ourselves just as we are, at the present moment, as the way to begin to discern God's will for us. No matter what the past, what the present, it is by accepting both that we are freed to move ahead.

In 1960 Thomas Merton wrote in a letter to L. P. Sabbath:

> The concrete existential situation you are in here and now, whatever it is, contains for you God's will, reality. Your only job is to accept it as it is, because it is the truth, not because it pleases you, gets you off the hook, or on a hook, or makes you feel safe....In order to do this you have to really believe deeply in God's love for you and see that even the "evil" in your life can serve the purpose of his love.

Merton is reminding us that the acceptance of God and the acceptance of ourselves (and the mystery of both) belong together.

In their book on prayer, *Primary Speech,* Ann and Barry Ulanov wrote in a similar vein:

> We must take ourselves as we find ourselves, and where we find ourselves, and make the best of it all. That means accepting the facts about ourselves—our fears and fantasies, our aggressions, our desires, our sexuality,

our spirituality. That means seeing what is positive, as well as what is not in our reality. That means accepting our reality and it means accepting and making full use of prayer as a guide to understanding reality.

Accepting our reality, of course, includes all kinds of things we may not have associated with prayer. It means accepting our parents (and sometimes grandparents if they have been influential in our lives). This is often easier said than done, for as Freud reminds us, "Parents never die." We have to deal with them until we are dead and—who knows?—perhaps for eternity.

I once asked a class I was teaching in spirituality to write brief papers each week in order to help them come to some deeper understanding of themselves. The papers were to be addressed to God. I didn't want to see them, but I hoped the students would be helped in this way to show themselves to God and thus to themselves.

The first assignment was to describe their mothers and fathers and their relationship to each other. This turned out to be a difficult assignment, particularly, I think, for the men. One forty-five-year-old man wrote:

> I thought I had long since laid to rest my struggles with my father, and now I am flooded once again with those bitter memories. I hope in writing God I have offered him all of that which I thought I had buried, but obviously have not.

Another student, aged sixty, wrote:

> My father died one morning when he was thirty-two and I was eight. The night before, as I was saying my prayers, I prayed that my father would die. I lived with that guilt for years and only recently have come to realize that many sons are in conflict with their fathers and that I have to accept God's forgiveness.

The point I want to make is simply that these early experiences of acceptance or rejection that arise in our earliest childhood and remain with us in one form or another—whether accepted or repressed—contain the seeds of our spiritual formation. That is, they form our predisposition to accepting the world and believing it is a good place to be or a hostile, frightening place. In the former, relationships are easier to establish; in the latter, they are more difficult. When the world is perceived as a good place, God often is seen as a benign creator; when the world is a frightening place, God is seen as hostile.

I am not trying to give you a psychological analysis of personality, but to point out the importance of accepting the past in order to accept the present. This includes all relationships, beginning with that of parent and child. Acceptance of all our relationships is a personal way of participating in the theology of justification by faith.

Our knowledge of ourselves and our knowledge of God intertwine. The author of *The Cloud of Unknowing* gave this advice to those seeking to know God:

> Strain every nerve in every possible way to know and experience yourself as you truly are. It will not be long, I suspect, before you have a real knowledge and experience of God as he is.

Our search for self-knowledge and knowledge of God is simply to cry, "*Abba,* Father." It is out of that inner conviction that we recognize "the Spirit bearing witness with our spirit that we are children of God, and if children, then heirs, heirs of God and joint heirs with Christ—if, in fact, we suffer with him that we may also be glorified with him" (Romans 8:16-17).

If it is true, as Phillips Brooks said, that "what is in the sermon must be in the preacher first," then the long-term preparation for preaching is preparing ourselves, while the short-term task is preparing the sermon. This long-term preparation is prayer. In the final analysis, the Spirit who bears witness with our spirit is the preacher, or informs the preacher. The sermon preached with the power of God will be so heard by those who themselves dwell in the Spirit. Paul put it this way:

> For the Spirit searches everything, even the depths of God. For what human being knows what is truly human except the human spirit that is within? So also no one comprehends what is truly God's except the Spirit of God. Now we have received not the spirit of the world, but the Spirit that is from God, so that we may understand the gifts bestowed on us by God. And we speak of these things in words not taught by human wisdom but taught by the Spirit, interpreting spiritual things to those who are spiritual. (1 Corinthians 2:10-13)

That is why silence, quiet, and prayer are indispensable in preparing to preach, for this is how the Spirit prepares us.

Silence is preparation for prayer; indeed, it *is* prayer. Waiting in God's presence and accepting our lives, just as they are, are all part of preparation for preaching. A sermon has to well up from within oneself, then the catalyst for preparing the sermon is the text. Slow down. Be quiet. Accept your situation. Wait. Then the text.

Perhaps the best way to summarize what I mean on this kind of prayer for the preacher is to quote a Japanese haiku found in Frederick Buechner's *Whistling in the Dark*. It goes like this:

> An old silent pond.
> Into the pond a frog jumps.
> Splash! Silence again.

A variant of this, designed for preaching, would read:

> A silent study.
> Into the study a text drops.
> Plop! Silence again.
> Then pray.

Prayer is response to God's initiative. In Saint Augustine's words, our hearts are restless until they rest in God, and God made us that way so that we might find our rest only in him.

Our prayer is the response of our entire life. It is attempting to do what we believe God wants us to do in all aspects of our life and in all the activities of that life. Preaching comes out of life and, therefore, the preacher must be involved in life. Participation in all aspects of life is one of the keys to prayer. No participation means no prayer; no prayer means no preaching—at least relevant preaching. Sabbaticals serving in soup kitchens are an important balance to sabbaticals spent in studies. The Incarnation is Christ everywhere, and our preaching Christ is being with him wherever.

How should we address God? Sometimes by saying nothing, by simply being present. Sometimes a mantra helps—a phrase or word that calls God to mind and heart. It is no accident, I think, that in Western culture many are finding that simply repeating the Eastern syllable *om* slows them down, centers them. "The object of theological work," wrote Karl Barth, "is not an it but a person," not some*thing* but some*one*.

Jesus said, "When you pray, say 'Father'." He might in another culture have told his disciples to say "Mother." In either case, he would have us address God as creator and helper. What image of God best helps you pray? The images at hand are numerous. Just one hymn from the Episcopal hymnal contains the images of God as Rock, Savior, Shepherd, Dove of Peace, and King; God is the God of might, the maker of the earth, sea and land, the one who cradles in one hand the heights and the depths; he is Father, Son, and Spirit.

In his letter to the Colossians, Paul wrote of Christ:

> He is the image of the invisible God, the firstborn of all creation; for in him all things in heaven and earth were created, things visible and invisible, whether thrones or dominions or rulers or powers—all things have been created through him and for him. He himself is before all things, and in him all things hold together. (Colossians 1:15-17)

That is why the simplest, most direct way to pray is to say, "Jesus." After that, say what is on your heart to say.

Words don't have to be spoken. Half-articulated (even half-baked!) thoughts will do. Sighs will do. "Aha" will do. Cries will do: "Christ, help me!" "For Christ's sake, help my friend." "Thank you" will do. So will "I am truly sorry, and I confess it to you right now." And so will "I love you, Jesus" or "I want to love you—help me to love you." Anything, in fact—*anything*—will do. What is on your heart, on your mind? Pour it out. "I believe, Lord; help my unbelief." That is prayer.

The key in all this seems to be trust and simplicity—utter simplicity. "You have to become a child again," Jesus reminded us. This is exactly what Jesus did in committing himself as a son to his Father. After he prophesied against the cities of Chorazin and Bethsaida, cities that saw his miracles yet still did not repent, Jesus declared,

> "I thank you, Father, Lord of heaven and earth, because you have hidden these things from the wise and the intelligent and have revealed them to infants; yes, Father, for such was your gracious will." (Matthew 11:25-26)

As a father knows a son, so also a son knows his father. It was out of that personal relation that Jesus carried out his mission, and likewise we his disciples on our mission. The key? Trust and simplicity. We are children of God, whose Spirit, joined to ours, assures us that we are his children.

There is one more general observation that is a consistent part of Christian devotion: the centrality of the Bible. The story of God is told in the history of Israel and in the life, death, and resurrection of Jesus Christ.

Preachers have to know that story so they can tell it to their people. This means to appropriate everything that biblical studies and biblical theology have come to mean in contemporary theological education. It includes biblical criticism, which, for people just beginning to study the Bible, might seem to destroy or weaken faith. On a second (or one hundredth) reading, however, biblical criticism opens the scriptures toward a deeper understanding of how the Christ of faith and Jesus of Nazareth belong together. Critical study and personal faith belong together. The Bible is read most penetratingly through the *eyes* of faith. This requires not only reason but imagination, intuition, and almost a poetic insight which makes it possible to take the Bible not literally, but seriously.

Meditating simply means thinking, but thinking with a certain spirit to enable one to get behind, or inside, scripture and the scenes described there. Probably the best-known pattern is found in the *Spiritual Exercises* of Ignatius of Loyola, where we are encouraged to enter into the scene described—the birth in the manger, a miracle, a healing, the foot of the cross—to try to discern the religious meaning for our own understanding and faith.

The Episcopal Church's prayer for this kind of assistance in interpreting scripture is the collect for the Sunday closest to November 16, during the season of Pentecost:

> Blessed Lord, who caused all holy Scriptures to be written for our learning: Grant us so to hear them, read, mark, learn, and inwardly digest them, that we may embrace and ever hold fast the blessed hope of everlasting life, which you have given us in our Savior Jesus Christ.

The key phrase, of course, is "inwardly digest." Brood over the meaning of the scene or text, chew it over, chop it up into small pieces, let it stay with you, sleep on it, dream about it.

Picture the scripture you're reading. Then *ponder* its meaning. We are to participate in the word or scene just as when we really look at a picture or painting we participate in it. The poet Rainer Maria Rilke commented that when we really *look* at a painting and think of what we see, we participate in some way in the painter's life. So we participate in the life of the author of the words, the painter of the scene. The word and the author are speaking to us, asking to participate in our life. That means—if we welcome them—change. We become different.

Then, what do you do in your own life to carry out its meaning? *Promise* to do something. Change something. What effect does the passage have on you? Once you know, *offer* it back to God—offer yourself back to God with the meaning of the text now part of you. If you have incorporated the text, your life will be changed in some way.

That is one form of meditating. There are others. A preacher should be familiar with them, should practice them regularly throughout his or her life, and should not hesitate to introduce the principle of meditation to all kinds of teaching, including sermons. Indeed, one effective form of sermon is taken from a biblical meditation designed to welcome the hearers inside the scene or passage.

You can, for example, pretend (a perfectly good word for any kind of prayer) that you are the boy at the picnic where Jesus fed the five thousand. How did you happen to be there? Were your parents present? Your friends? When the talking stopped and the people wanted to be fed, who asked you for your picnic lunch? Did Jesus? Or one of his disciples? Was it easy to do, or were you a little hesitant to give it up? Who distributed that food? How did you feel about its being given away and apparently never used up? How did the gathering end? Did Jesus ever come over to thank you? How did you feel? What were your thoughts as you walked back home? Did you think you would ever see him again? Did your heart ache?

Prayer helps a scripture text take on life. If it is read, marked, and inwardly digested, the preacher draws on its life and so will the congregation.

The significance of preaching is not so much the accuracy of interpretation of the scripture text as it is the impression it makes upon the hearers, whether anything happens to them in their lives. James Carr, in *The Silence of God,* wrote:

> Great interpreters are not persons who have found the true meaning of the text and set it out so clearly and persuasively that all further interpretation is unnecessary. Great interpreters are those who inspire others to voice their own response to the text; who enable others to say what they had never known it possible to say.

Kierkegaard meant much the same thing when he compared people in church to the actors in a liturgical drama, while the preacher is the prompter who facilitates the drama.

You often have to let yourself go in this kind of prayer. It is not a rational, objective, analytical process; it is, rather, part of your journey in faith and therefore you have to be willing to be intuitive, non-rational, imaginative. It can be the catalyst for a deepened understanding of God and the mysterious movement of God's Spirit in Christ in our relationships. It doesn't hurt at all to be a little "far out" in imagining Christ's presence in prayer and his engaging you in conversation.

The setting may not be a hot day near a well in Samaria. It may be a cold day in New England as the mist begins to rise shortly after dawn. Dark tree trunks stand starkly against the snow and ice, rising up from patches of brown. Christ asks for water, from me, of all people. He knows "all I ever did"—what kind of mysterious knowledge is this, to be divinely known by a stranger walking over the snow? So what did the woman at the Samarian well do? She went out and told others and they came and then they left and said to her: "It is no longer because of what you said that we believe, for we have heard for ourselves, and we know that this is truly the Savior of the world" (John 4:42). Likewise, the preacher has to preach out of personal experience and knowledge of the one who knows "all I ever did." Then the hearers of the Word will hear the Christ for themselves. They will know who Jesus is and therefore who they are.

That kind of preaching is prayer. It comes out of personal knowledge, the kind of preacher Thomas Carlyle was seeking when he said, "We are looking for a preacher who knows God and not by hearsay."

Now how does this personal knowledge of God grow? It is difficult to generalize, but let me try to describe what I believe tends to happen. After we have participated in "acts of prayer," such as I have been describing above, for some length of time (I cannot translate "some length of time" into calendar time because it varies so), after prayer has become incorporated into our being as part of our nature, we begin to sense that if we will be content simply to pay attention to God, God will increasingly take on the direction of our life, including our prayer life. Gradually we do less and less, and God does more and more. Or so it seems. It is true that we have to work out our own salvation with fear and trembling; and it is also true that God is at work in us "both to will and to work for his good pleasure" (Philippians 2:13).

This is what happens, I believe, when people talk of God being the best spiritual director. God is the one who tells us what's what in our spiritual lives, where we are off the track and in what direction we should go. This is not to deny the importance of "soul friends" or those with whom we can share "the deep things of God." We all need someone for sharing, for confession perhaps, for simple spiritual friendship, for consultation when we run into road blocks and need special help. But it is essentially God who directs.

We are moved in this level of prayer to see how it is that God the Holy Spirit is the One who is praying through us, and we are simply participating in the prayer of the Spirit. As Paul writes in his letter to the Romans, "When we cry, 'Abba! Father!' it is that very Spirit bear-

ing witness with our spirit that we are children of God"
(8:16). In the same letter Paul compares the Spirit to an
intercessor dwelling deep within us and praying for us
"with sighs too deep for words" (8:26).

God is trying through all the experiences of life—the
good and the bad, the happy and the tragic, the uplifting
and the degrading—to transform us into Christ-likeness.
God's Spirit moves through all creation, and we are invited, enticed, called to join with that Spirit through the
crosses we experience of pain, loss, suffering, guilt, and
death, as well as through joy-filled experiences of grace,
faith, hope, love, and fulfillment. All through the process
of living we are being led to trust him who is behind and
hidden in all the experiences and images we have of
him. "Even though our outward nature is wasting away,"
Paul wrote to the Corinthians, "our inner nature is being
renewed day by day" (2 Corinthians 4:16).

Some of the characteristics of this renewal, this transformation, are, first of all, we don't try so hard. We don't
press so hard to make our way to God, don't take ourselves (either our virtues or our sins) quite so seriously.
We are willing to give up control over ourselves—as
though we were in charge of our destiny! We become
more willing to let life be life as it ebbs and flows, and less
anxious about whether we are getting our way or not, or
going in the direction we determine we should go in.

Karl Rahner once wrote that his only absolute cer-
tainty about God was that he knew he was his. When I
know that I belong to God, I am not so eager to talk
about "my" life as something that is mine to do with as I
want, and I begin to see that my life is really a gift to me
from God. It is his life. It is a gift entrusted to me, but
what happens to it is more his doing than my own. This
means, I believe, that we sit a little more lightly as to
how life progresses or improves, remains static, or even

retrogresses. We are given a little distance from it and are no longer so obsessed by it. Questions like New York Mayor Koch's famous one-liner, "How'm I doing?" seem more and more irrelevant.

Our struggles and our sins still continue, of course, but we come increasingly to realize that more significant than these are faith, hope, and love, that these are gifts that God wants us to have (and that we already have), so we need most of all simply to wait upon him, to be drawn more into him. We are more content to leave all these struggles to God and trust him to do what he will with them. It is now not so much our business as his. We are increasingly aware that what we want, God wants—our transformation into Christ—and we know full well that we can't do that by ourselves. Only God can. So we trust him. Christ's purpose is to transform our nature into his for, as has been said, "he became human that we may become divine."

Another way of putting this is to say that we are no longer *seeking* God; we are *learning* God. It is as though we think that we have to seek God when we begin this pilgrimage, but gradually we come to see that our seeking him is really his seeking us. Once we understand that, then the rest of our journey is learning him. He is the teacher. It is not so much learning his ways, although those lessons continue. It is, rather, learning *him*. Just as teachers teach themselves as well as their discipline, so God teaches himself as well as his ways. We learn *him* as well as what he *wants*. Lady Julian of Norwich put it this way: "Desire we our Lord and He shall lerne us."

God is now perceived not so much as creator—out there and sometimes over against us, the one upon whom we are dependent and to whom we confess—but more as a friend, one who wishes us well, who wants to draw us closer to him, to deepen our friendship. Finally we begin to see him as a lover who wants (as lovers always do) to become one with those he loves.

This brings us to the threshold of mystical prayer, where God and his children are joined in union. Many people think this kind of prayer is beyond them; they do not claim to be mystics and do not or cannot cultivate mystical prayer. It belongs, they think, to those special saints whose vocation is a life of prayer. But I am not persuaded that this is true.

Contemplative prayer is, I believe, the prayer of many persons (including preachers) who may not know how to label it. The experience of being one with God in our lives—or, more properly, God being one with our lives—is a reality today as in other days. It is "I yet not I" who is the Christ within. The union of the "I" and Christ is God's gift, not our creation. We can but wait upon him that he may do what he wills.

But what we can do is enter fully into the Spirit, who draws us closer to God and who enables us to pray with the mind of Christ. If our vocation is to preach, it will be this Christ whom we preach through our life of prayer, the crucified Christ in whose life we are hidden, for we have been crucified with him. And if we have been crucified with him, then we are risen with him. That means our preaching will be in the power of the resurrection. It will be Christ preached, and we will do it with our whole being. Then God can do what he wills as his Spirit is given to those who hear. It is up to them and God. We can forget it and begin to think about next week's sermon.

I am tempted at this juncture to make an appeal for a more sympathetic understanding of mysticism, which has always been on the fringe of theological study. Most of us have in our own lives been influenced by the mystics of the West, a wonderful roll call from Paul, Augustine, and Aquinas over the centuries to Teilhard de Chardin, Thomas Merton, William Johnston, and Matthew Fox. I think also more personally of Alan Whittemore of the Order of the Holy Cross, who was of great help to me. Toward the end of his life he summed up in his spiritual journal what he had come to believe:

> My quiet conviction is that the real thing that we want is to be one with God....And we *are* one with Him in the sense that whether we are good or bad, joyful or sorrowing, aware or unaware of His nearness, He in his great love has united Himself with us and undergoes the experiences of *every* one of us, moment by moment.

I believe that. It is very difficult for any person who has had even the slightest mystical experience to explain anything about it except to those who have had similar ones. In *Divine Landscapes* Ronald Blythe wrote:

> It is always hard even for mystics to describe precisely what they see. St. John of the Cross wrote:
> > "The farther that I climbed the height
> > The less I seemed to understand
> > The Cloud so tenebrous and grand
> > That there illuminates the night."

It must also be said that if you consider yourself to be a mystic or informed by mystical experience, you do not need someone else to tell you about it or what you should do or where you are to go. You and God are on your own. He will take you with him, united to him. Trust him.

Let me conclude with a prayer of Thomas Merton, who knew a thing or two about the essence of mystical prayer.

> My Lord God,
> I have no idea where I am going.
> I do not see the road ahead of me.
> I cannot know for certain where it will end.
> Nor do I really know myself,
>   and the fact that I think that I am following your will
>   does not mean that I am actually doing so.
> But I believe that the desire to please you
>   does in fact please you.
> And I hope that I will never do anything
>   apart from that desire.
> And I know that if I do this,
>   you will lead me by the right road
>   though I may know nothing about it.
> Therefore, I will trust you always
>   though I may seem lost
>   and in the shadow of death.
> I will not fear, for you are forever with me,
>   and you will never leave me
>   to face my troubles alone.

So take heart. Go to your text. Begin to "read, mark, learn, and inwardly digest" it, which means simply to pray it. God will help you. Stay close to him. Continue to learn him. Desire him and he will "lerne" you. You will be all right!

Paradox

If you and I can always carry this double consciousness, that we are messengers and that we are witnesses, we shall have in our preaching all the authority and independence of assured truth, and yet all the appeal and convincingness of personal belief.

— Phillips Brooks —

I n my first chapter I talked about grace as the gift of God, the assurance of God, the sense of being in tune with God, of being one with him. Next I talked about prayer and how prayer brings us to respond to God with our whole life. Now I want to look at some of life's experiences as they are understood through prayer and as they are related to God and to God's grace. I have called this chapter "Paradox," but it could also be called "The Preacher as Pastor." The purpose of this is to make clear that clergy are not (and ought not) to be exempt from any of life's experiences, and to consider how the experiences may be preparing the pastor to preach.

A student once asked Dr. George Buttrick in homiletics class where he got illustrations for his sermons. Buttrick came right back with, "Everywhere!" At the time I didn't believe it, but I hope he will accept what I say now as an apology and will forgive me for my skepticism.

The range of experiences most of us go through in our everyday lives might be categorized in three ways: as paradox, loss, and joy. First, paradox.

A few years ago a savings bond that my wife and I held came due. What should we do with the five thousand dollars? Not being well informed in the world of finance, I consulted a friend who is a "financial counselor," although in an earlier day he would have been called simply a stockbroker. So I asked him what I should do to invest the money. "Well, I will tell you," he replied, "but first I want to pass on to you a motto I learned from my father, who also dealt in stocks and bonds. His motto was, 'Your guess is as good as mine.'" After he had told me his suggestion (which was "Roll it over"—a new phrase for me), he asked me: "Now, in your profession, do you have a motto?"

I had never thought about it until that moment, but I replied, "Yes, I do. It is this: 'You never can tell.'"

You never can tell what's going to happen. You can say, "This marriage will last no more than two years, but that one will last forever," or, "That student is going to succeed and make a mark on the world, but that one will never make it." Or you can say, "This is the year for the Red Sox." But things don't always turn out the way we predict. Marriages turn out just the opposite way, students upset all our predictions—and as for the Red Sox, no year, it seems, is ever theirs.

When it comes to charting one's career through life, it usually doesn't turn out the way we predict, either. Write down your life's goals on a piece of paper, then tear it up and throw it away. Your life will turn out differently. "You never can tell"—that's my life's motto. Life is too unpredictable, too chancy, too much of a gamble to make predictions. When my bishop ordained me, he said, "John, I'm going to take a chance on you." Not exactly the most encouraging word, but a realistic one, whether for decisions on ordinations or most anything else. You never can tell.

Life is shot through with ambiguities, contradictions, chances, ambivalences. It is shot through with paradox. This is especially true when we take seriously the Christian claim that Christ makes all things new. For if Christ makes all things new, we had better not be too absolute in stating what is going to happen.

The race goes to the fastest runner? Well, the first shall be last and the last first. An honest day's wages for an honest day's work? Well, the laborer who worked three hours in the late afternoon shade gets the same wage as the one who worked twelve hours bearing the heat and burden of the day. You want to save your life? Well, you save it by giving it away. When you're dead, you're dead? Well, Christ is raised from the dead. As in Adam, all die? So also in Christ shall all be made alive.

Saint Paul also spoke of paradox. "Work out your own salvation with fear and trembling," he wrote to the Philippians, "for it is God who is at work in you, enabling you both to will and to work for his good pleasure" (2:12-13). "When I want to do what is good, evil lies close at hand," he reminded the young church at Rome. "For I delight in the law of God in my inmost self, but I see in my members another law at war with the law of my mind, making me captive to the law of sin that dwells in my members" (7:21-23). But Paul's most striking statement of paradox is found in his second letter to the Corinthians, where he speaks of the paradox of discipleship:

> We are treated as impostors, and yet are true; as unknown, and yet are well known; as dying, and see—we are alive; as punished, and yet not killed; as sorrowful, yet always rejoicing; as poor, yet making many rich; as having nothing, and yet possessing everything. (2 Corinthians 6:8b-10)

The greatest paradox of all, of course, is that Christ is both God and man. All Christian paradoxes rise from this central one. How can this be? In his *Concluding Unscientific Postscript,* Søren Kierkegaard wrote that paradox emerges when "eternal truth" and human existence are placed together:

> Christianity has declared itself to be the eternal essential
> truth which has come into being in time. It has pro-
> claimed itself the Paradox and it has required of the indi-
> vidual the inwardness of faith.

This "inwardness of faith" by grace holds all the ambiguities, contrarieties, and paradoxes together. It is that
which makes the tensions bearable and frees the Spirit to
move us on through those tensions.

Psychiatrist Gerald May says much the same thing in
Will and Spirit:

> For Christians, the prime example of "both/and" is found
> in Jesus himself. Christian orthodoxy holds that Jesus
> was *both* human *and* divine, but the words and actions
> of Jesus are more revealing than any theological inter-
> pretations. Of all things, Jesus did not minimize his hu-
> manity. He spoke of God as Father in a way that clearly
> saw God as other, even to the point of feeling forsaken
> by God. Nothing could be more grounded in human
> separateness than this. But he also could say, "I and the
> Father are one....The Father is in me, and I in the Father."

Christ, the first-born of all creation, came to restore
the harmony of his broken creation. This is known by
those who, again in Kierkegaard's phrase, possess the
"inwardness of faith." What is required of us as followers
of Christ is to "continue securely established and steadfast in the faith, without shifting from the hope promised
by the gospel" (Colossians 1:23). We need to pray to
help restore the harmony broken in us, as the seventeenth-century priest and poet John Donne prayed:

> These distempers, thou only, O God,
>   who are true, and perfect harmony,
> canst tune and rectify
>   and set in order again.

As a preacher, you will be preaching to a congregation of men and women who are filled with both grace and paradox, whole selves and shattered selves. In other words, they have the same nature that you do. The power that comes from the preacher, the help that the sermon provides in assisting people to put the pieces of their lives back together again—or at least to keep them from falling into complete disarray—will depend in large measure on the extent to which the one who preaches is living that "inwardness of faith." That is done through one's trust in God and through responding to God in faith. How one does that is one's prayer.

Because people and preacher share the same broken-ness and grace, the preacher must be content to live with paradoxes and ambiguities in his or her own life, and not attempt to resolve them or impose solutions upon the congregation. When this happens, the preacher accepts the fact that he or she is at the same time a sinner and a sinner justified. Grace is trusted to be more powerful, more true to one's essential nature, than all the division and strife we bear. This is the proclamation that Christ's Gospel is a Gospel of hope. Therefore the preacher does not have to be in charge of the people in the congregation; they belong to God. The preacher's task is to set them free to be themselves in their own understanding of the Gospel.

"Conflict management," for example, is a popular concept in the churches today. However useful it might be for providing techniques leading to consensus in times of conflict, conflict can be managed finally only by the Holy Spirit. Once either the preacher or the congregation attempts to manage the other, the Christian struggle is lost. When one side presses for victory over the other, there are no winners, only losers. I have often heard parishioners complain about rectors who keep pushing them to agree with his or her ideas and opinions. "Pushing" is not the same as "challenging": "challenging" is presenting the Gospel, not one's own opinions.

There can be no coercion to accept the Gospel, but there can be persuasion. The only persuasion that persuades, finally, is the persuasion of love: the concern for the good of the other. To embrace the Gospel is to embrace one another and to stay together so that the Holy Spirit may do the persuading. This involves faith and risk, and it may not always work in the pragmatic sense. But when the model for this risk-taking is the preacher—both in preaching and in living—it is worth the risk.

Conflicts, then, may not always be resolved, but they will be bearable. The church can still go forward, perhaps stumbling and falling down, but always picking itself up and going on, not sure about much of anything except trust, love, and grace, doing its best to "continue securely established and steadfast in the faith, without shifting from the hope promised by the gospel" (Colossians 1:23).

Amidst all the ambiguities, conflicts, and paradoxes of the Christian life, it is in the final analysis grace alone that enables the preacher and the people to stay together. Grace—the willingness not to try to be in control but to trust the Spirit—strengthens both preacher and people to be loyal to the One who paradoxically *died* in order to give us *life*. In his embrace of the cross in response to his Father, Jesus set the Spirit free so that we might respond to one another in love as the way we can best respond to him. It is that response—faithfulness and love—that is Christian prayer. It is so for the preacher; it is so for all of us. We have paradox upon paradox, grace upon grace, all held together by faith and prayer.

The paradoxical nature of our sinful existence and God's love held together by Christ was put this way by Julian of Norwich, the well-loved fourteenth-century mystic and anchorite:

> Love was your Lord's meaning.
> Just as God is truly our Father
>   so also is God truly our Mother.
> God said: It is necessary
>   that sin should exist
> But all will be well, and all will be well
>   and every manner of thing will be well.

How can we develop such a spirit? How will we live it? How will we communicate it? How can we belong to such a spirit so that we can pray it? Make it our own? Saint Paul wrote that the Spirit

> helps us in our weakness; for we do not know how to pray as we ought, but that very Spirit intercedes for us with sighs too deep for words. And God, who searches the heart, knows what is the mind of the Spirit, because the Spirit intercedes for the saints according to the will of God. (Romans 8:26-27)

How does the Spirit "help us in our weakness"? How does it "intercede for us with sighs too deep for words"? The Spirit may indeed lift our spirits with the delight of sunrises and sunsets, and we may be "surprised by joy," in C. S. Lewis's words, but the Spirit encounters us more profoundly in experiences of loss and pain and what we often refer to as our "crosses." Our theology is formed out of those experiences, as we ourselves are formed. They are Christ transforming us.

If the preacher is to bring the hope and strength of the Gospel to the people of the congregation, he or she must also be their pastor. It is inconceivable that the saving Word can be preached without knowing from what it is that people—including the preacher—have to be saved from: losses, diminishments, sin, death. It is through the bitter experiences of loss that we come to a deeper understanding of what faith means, and this rises out of our prayers in the face of loss. We agonize over the agonies of our people as well as our own, and out of that prayer we are given at least glimpses of hope and assurances of the Gospel's saving power. "True prayer," wrote Kierkegaard, "is a struggle with God in which one triumphs through the triumph of God." How can we be aligned with that triumph except through faith and prayer? "With sighs too deep for words"?

Sermons are a struggle. It is not simply because they are often difficult to prepare, although that is true, but because they are created out of the pain of a preacher and pastor living and struggling alongside his or her people to find meaning (and therefore hope) in all the experiences of life—not only the painful experiences of others we observe in our ministry, but those we live through ourselves. How do we make sense out of both "bad things happening to good people" and "good things happening to bad people" when we *are* those people, both good and bad?

Obviously life is jagged and seldom smooth, broken and not often whole. Breakage, loss, separation, and death are part and parcel of living and loving. Poet William Blake put it this way in "Auguries of Innocence":

> Man was made for joy and woe;
> And, when this we rightly know,
>   Safely through the world we go.
> Joy and woe are woven fine,
>   A clothing for the soul divine.

How can we account for the fact that so many of the people who seem to make the most out of life are those who have suffered much pain? Why is it that the alcoholic is helped most by recovering alcoholics? Why do people who mourn receive greatest strength from those who have already mourned? Why do we instinctively turn to persons who have been broken when we ourselves are breaking?

For example, a nineteenth-century British philosopher, J. R. Illingworth, wrote, "The men of sorrows are the men of influence. Even more than knowledge, pain is power." Wordsworth spoke of the "deep distress" that "humanized" his soul. Thornton Wilder wrote, "In love's service only the wounded may serve." Dean Inge, commenting on the death of his daughter, wrote: "Bereavement is the deepest initiation into the mystery of divine love, more revealing and profound than even mutual happy human love." A mother, reflecting upon the sudden death of her son, wrote some years afterward, "Suddenly my life has descended onto a deeper level and my heart keeps singing all the time." And a father, after committing his teen-aged daughter to a mental institu-

tion, said, "I shall never say an unkind word about any-
body for the rest of my life."

What is going on here? We have come to a Christian
theology that can be preached by living and praying
about our living, by living with our people and praying
with and for them. We may not be able to explain to a
mother why God has let her daughter commit suicide,
but we can hold her hand as we sit on the steps of the
morgue waiting for the autopsy to be completed.

So our living as pastors with our people goes along
with our theology. There is our "thinking the truth" in order that we may "do the truth," but it is in doing the
truth that we discover the truth. "The one who knows
my will is the one who does it," Jesus told his disciples.
To adapt a phrase of Henri Nouwen's, preachers are
healers who have themselves been wounded.

There is a strength for life that is hidden under the sur-
face, and that erupts especially through brokenness and
suffering and death. We know that spirit, are strengthened by it, are given courage for life by the people who
have been broken. From their broken lives comes a
strength for our life. It is a mysterious spirit that seems to
be embedded right at the heart of the universe to bring
life to people of all kinds: Jews, Christians, atheists,
Communists; all people forever, eternal, universal. Christians say we recognize Christ where we are and especially where we are broken.

God redeemed the world *through* Christ's suffering.
He took the cross for his love of God, and power was
then unleashed throughout the world by his Spirit, which
we call holy. It is as though Christ asked God, "How is
your will going to get done?" And God answered, "As
you are willing to be obedient to my love and show it
forth, even unto death on the cross!" It was the worst
suffering and the greatest innocence. God made him to

be sin who knew no sin, and in the breaking of his body he broke the power of sin. God's act of redemption was accomplished through the cross, through the suffering of the Son who took it to express God's will as love.

The cross did not *change* God's mind. It *expressed* God's mind: it is love. God's will is love. That love is more powerful than anything else in the world. More powerful than sin. More powerful than death.

Christ is raised from the dead. Love lives. The power of love is set loose in the world to redeem, reconcile, bring people closer to one another and to God. This is Easter, the Gospel of the resurrection. The Good News of the cross is the new life of Easter.

At the heart of God's love there is always, therefore, what von Hügel called a "costingness." Atoning love has power because it costs so much. If love is cheap, it doesn't have any power to move us. Love you can buy for money has no strength. The greater the cost of love, the greater the power. The love of God for us cost him his Son. That is how much he loved us.

Apparently God shows his love best when we go through our worst. And every time we take our suffering for the love of God we participate in his continuing act of redemption. You ask God, "How are you going to get your will done in me?" He answers, "As you are willing to take your sufferings, trusting in my love." That is the way of the cross.

Saint Paul, who had his share of suffering, wrote: "We know that all things work together for good for those who love God" (Romans 8:28). This is true even in our most painful experiences: if we accept them, trusting that God has a purpose for them, offer them back to God, and then get on with our living, we discover not simply that strength for living comes to us, but also that we strengthen others—more accurately, that God strength-

ens others through us. We somehow share in his atoning
work. We triumph through his triumph. This does not, of
course, explain the mystery of suffering, but it can help
us enter into the most profound mystery of life and there
find strength.

On his deathbed, the seventeenth-century Puritan,
Thomas Hooker, said: "I am at peace with all men and
[God] is at peace with me, and from that assurance I feel
that inward joy which this world can neither give nor
take from me."

It was for the joy that was set before him that Christ
endured the cross; that was the way in which he could
do his Father's will. We share in that joy as we take up
our crosses and follow him—or try to.

So the question is: is that what we want to do? If to do
God's will is what we really want, then things work out,
somehow. If we don't, then it's all over—that is, the
search for meaning is over, and we give up and die.

Wanting to conform to the will of God is responding
to life, to God, in obedience to love. That means the
cross, death to self-will, death to obsession with one's
own ego trying to maintain control of life, death to con-
stant self-expression, self-indulgence. This kind of dying
is at the heart of living because loving is what makes living. This is the Gospel.

God is where we are. Do we want him there? If the
answer is yes, then our response to him is really his. We
then participate in his response, begin to die to ourselves
and truly to live. Our prayer, then, is not trying to *get*

something but to *be with* Someone and hence to become someone. Who we become finally is our sermon.

Prayer is *now*. It rises out of this moment, in everything, right now. Karl Rahner put it this way in his *Encounters with Silence:*

> If You have given me no single place to which I can flee and be sure of finding You, if anything I do can mean the loss of You, then I must be able to find You in every place, in each and every thing I do. Otherwise I couldn't find You at all, and this cannot be, since I can't possibly exist without You. Thus I must seek You in all things. If every day is "everyday," then every day is *Your* day, and every hour is the hour of *Your* grace....
>
> God comes to us continually, both directly and indirectly. He demands of us both work and pleasure, and wills that each should not be hindered, but rather strengthened, by the other. Thus the interior man possesses his life in both these ways, in activity and in rest. And he is whole and undivided in each of them, for he is entirely in God when he joyfully rests, and he is entirely in himself when he actively loves.

The Spirit of Jesus Christ, then, reveals the love of God to us in *all* the experiences of life, and we respond to him in his Spirit through all the experiences of life. That is prayer, and that is prayer for the preacher. The illustrations for this kind of preaching come, as Dr. Buttrick said, "from everywhere."

One final word about loss. Among the losses that human beings undergo—and preachers are not exempt—is the loss of faith. What do preachers do when the Word of God escapes them? Faith at its best makes it possible to discern the God who is always hidden, always silent. But when faith has gone, God has gone—and so, often, does prayer. And when prayer goes, so does faith. Often God has gone and the reason we cannot find him is that we do not obey him or want to obey him. Our lives, our moral lives, help us lose him. They may also help us find him again.

The question is: do you want to find him? If the answer is yes, the only way to find him is to trust life, love your neighbor (or your spouse, your child, your friend), and by faith give yourself to the God hidden behind life's experiences, who is so strangely silent. You decide if that is what you want. The decision is yours. Such a decision is, in fact, prayer: it is prayer for faith. And it will be answered if it is genuine prayer. Karl Barth wrote:

> God hears *genuine* prayer. And the criterion of genuineness of this prayer is that it will be made in certainty that it will be heard....The certainty that this petition will be heard is consequently also the certainty in which theological work should be courageously started and performed.

"Theological work" for our purpose is simply to get on with preparing the sermon. Pray and work. *Ora et labora.* In retrospect it will seem to be grace. Live it as a gift from God; it will turn out to be grace. Then preach. Preach faith. Preach trust. Preach love. Live it as well as you are able. The people will hear you gladly. Or at least they will hear you.

In speaking of her conversion to Roman Catholicism, Clare Booth Luce described a sense of the Presence suddenly coming to her in this way:

> I find it difficult to explain what did happen. I expect that the easiest thing is to say that *something was.* My whole soul was cleft clean by it, as a silk veil slit by a shining sword. And I *knew.* I do not know now what I knew. I remember, I didn't know even then. That is, I didn't know with any "faculty." It was not in my mind or heart or bloodstream. But whatever it was I knew, it was something that made enormous sense....Then joy abounded in all of me. Or rather I abounded in joy. I seemed to have no nature, and yet my whole nature was adrift in this immense joy, as a speck of dust is seen to dance in a great golden shaft of sunlight.

This is one of those mysterious events that overtake, overwhelm us at times. They are epiphanies of the divine amidst the ordinary; I have heard them called "minor ecstasies." They come from out of the blue, unasked for and inexplicable, simply glorious. We can't account for these kinds of mysterious gifts except as gifts of grace from the God we don't know very much about. C. S. Lewis's phrase, "surprised by joy" describes it perfectly. A divine Presence engulfs us unexpectedly and we abound in joy.

To be engulfed in this kind of joy can be a prelude to conversion, as it was for Clare Booth Luce. We can be grateful for the joy in such experiences as these, and can thank the mysterious Giver for such gifts. We can, of course, also shrug such experiences off as having no meaning beyond indigestion, perhaps, or a guilty conscience seeking compensation, or simply a projection from deep in our psyche. But accepting them as "showings" of the divine Presence hovering around may be the introduction to an inward journey leading to Christ—indeed, initiated by Christ, who turns out to be the way himself.

When Christ is our companion, he leads us to a deeper, more profound joy which, strangely enough, does not come out of "glorious" experiences but out of painful ones—devastating, destructive, deadly ones. I am referring, of course, to that joy that rises from the cross. In the words of the collect for Monday in Holy Week:

> Almighty God, whose most dear Son went not up to joy but first he suffered pain, and entered not into glory before he was crucified: Mercifully grant that we, walking in the way of the cross, may find it none other than the way of life and peace.

We preach Christ crucified so that our people may have some sense of the power of the resurrection and the joy that is given to those who are united with Christ in both crucifixion and resurrection. We preach it best when we ourselves have accepted the crosses given us as from God himself, and have experienced the joy that then is given.

This is experienced death and experienced joy. It happens when we can say of ourselves: "I have been at the bottom of the abyss, where there was nothing to hold on to—no love, no support, no hope, but I embraced it all and was raised from the dead." This kind of joy comes with a life that is carried on to the best of one's ability, with the faith or confidence that this is what one is meant to do. This is why the people of joy always seem to be those who have gone through the worst and whose confidence is no longer in themselves but in the Christ who has been with them in their sufferings, losses, and pains, their failures and death.

It is the crosses that people bear in life that they need help with. That is why—whether they know it con- sciously or not—most of them are in church in the first place. How to make sense of the pains, the losses, the breakings, and the apparent meaninglessness at certain times of their lives? Well, that is when the Gospel preached by those who know the saving power of Christ is heard. That is when, through the sermon, peace and joy descend and begin to envelop those who, by the Spirit dwelling within them, have ears to hear. It hap- pens when the preacher does not so much know peace but *is* peace, does not merely know joy, but *is* joy. How do we come to preach peace and joy? Only as we come to know it, live it—or try to live it—and come to experi- ence without any doubt the power of Christ that saves.

And how do we go about getting all this? I am tempted to say, "God only knows," but I don't want to appear frivolous. What I will say is, if you know God, you will know. It involves personal, interior knowledge for your own life in God, dealing with the experiences and crosses in your life. All you have to do is live your life as fully, wholly, and completely as you can as a Christian. You don't have to look around for crosses. They will come as part and parcel of life as you go about your business of trying to love God with all your heart and soul and mind and your neighbor as yourself, and involve yourself in trying to redress the wrongs in this world.

If you live in faith and live in love, responding to God through everything that comes, you will be living a life of prayer. And when you do that—listening for God, paying attention to what God is doing, offering yourself to him, he will give you everything you need, for he will be giving you *himself.* Then just be yourself. Get the text. Pray and work. Pray and prepare. Then go preach.

Vocation

*Never sacrifice your reverence for truth
to your desire for usefulness. Say nothing
which you do not believe to be true
because you think it may be helpful.*

— Phillips Brooks —

I n this final chapter I want to return once more to the central theme of prayer, and then I want to turn to consider prayer in the place where the preachers are prepared, which is in community, usually in a seminary community.

I hope my theme is clear by now: the preacher is a Christian person who prays, not simply when he or she is preparing a sermon, but all the time, in all experiences of life. Preaching is not so much an art form as it is a *profession*, and it is not so much a profession as it is a *vocation*, just as the ministry is. If a person is called by God to preach and the sermon is a response to God as well as to those who hear it, then the Word of God is preached. It hinges in the first instance upon the preacher and his or her prayers, and in the final analysis it depends upon God.

To "put on Christ" means that our nature is continually being transformed into Christ's nature. That personal growth and transformation will be reflected in the preaching. We should be preaching somewhat differently at the end of our ministry than at the beginning; we are preaching the same Gospel, but *we* have changed. As Phillips Brooks put it, "The truth has not changed, but you have grown to fuller understanding of it, to larger capacity for receiving and transmitting it." That principle is the same for the preacher as for any leader in the business or professional or artistic world. As time goes on, we have increased ability and development of skills, a broader understanding of the values inherent in the work, and a deeper commitment to the enterprise of which we are a part.

The inspiring teacher is revered not so much for mastery of the subject as for the strength of his or her commitment to it. The teacher teaches a subject, to be sure, but more than that, he or she teaches—communicates—him or herself. It is that spirit of devotion to the discipline that leaves the lasting impression upon the students, so that we remember the teacher long after we have forgotten the subject. In a similar way, we remember the integrity of the preacher and a personal commitment to the Gospel longer than the words of any particular sermon.

To put the matter directly: preaching at its best is done by God the Holy Spirit. The Spirit will preach through the mind, voice, vision, personality, and hard work of the preacher, of course, but if it is the Spirit informing these human factors, then it is God preaching. And those who have ears to hear will hear. There is the *message* given and there is the *witness* lived. The message of the Gospel will always be the same: Christ. Our witness to it will change as we change. The key is our living to the best of our ability in response to his Spirit and in living in his Spirit. Then God preaches.

Since God has chosen us, we choose him; we choose to be chosen. Prayer is choosing to be with God. We choose to be present to the One who is always present to Christ, who is always present to us.

Recently I had the opportunity to meet on a weekly basis for six weeks with clergy who are already at the midpoint of their ministries as pastors. I asked them a question: What do you think you need now most of all? Here are some of their answers.

> I believe that I am at a point in my life where I will stagnate as a Christian, as a pastor, as a husband, as a father (and in all of the relationships of which I am a part) if my spiritual life is not stretched, strengthened, and deepened. More time, imagination, and hard work need to be expended to create intimacy with the Lord in order that I may become what in baptism I am called to be.

> I think I have learned how to think theologically....I hope now to start to learn to think spiritually.

> I find myself yearning for a deeper relationship with God, having the need for quiet time with God and the desire for a more structured, intentional spiritual life....All of this hopefully is the work of the Lord stirring within, but also may be related to moving toward fifty years of age and changes in personal life with children going off to college and my wife entering the work world for the first time.

> I wish to develop an adequate interior life, a discerning capability to know the will of God, how to become spiritually sensitive to God's guidance and the spiritual needs of my fellow brothers and sisters.

I am mentally, physically, and spiritually tired. There is a strong tug to withdraw—to rest and be quiet—to indulge in long periods of retreat and reading and prayer. I begin to think that this is a genuine direction from the Holy Spirit, with the warning that this withdrawal not be so complete that I lose touch with the community or with the parish I serve.

Right now I am wondering about the future. Will I feel close to myself then? Closer to God?

All of this sounds very familiar. How can preachers have any opportunity to develop any peace of mind or soul—any prayer life—in the midst of the busy, hectic life of the parish?

The issue here is: how is our personal conviction about our *vocation* to be maintained? Probably more than any other issue, this is the one which lies at the heart of the spiritual life of the minister and determines whether his or her spirit remains alive and vital or dries up and dies, whether it continues to mature or becomes stunted.

Two ways by which spiritual maturity is developed are through *conflict* and through *decision-making*. We live at a time in which church or congregational conflict is surfacing more frequently, evidence of some kind of restlessness of spirit. Conflicts are no longer hidden or simply endured. There is a new discipline of managing conflict, with a new category of literature to describe it.

One such book is called *Preaching Through a Storm* by H. B. Hicks, Jr. After the author describes some of the battles he has been through, he asks himself what he has learned. He decides that if he had it to do all over again, he would have concentrated more on his life of prayer, since the needs of the self suffer the most neglect in a turbulent situation, and "a spirit-fed and spirit-filled mind is an absolute essential if responsible and serious preaching is to take place in the storm situation." Hicks goes on to ask, "How do you preach when your enemies are present?"—meaning, I suppose, the agents of conflict in the parish. "Your people are your teachers,...your professors in the pews." To pray for them, to lift them into God's presence, to be bound together with them in God, is a condition required for the beginning of conflict resolution. We are bound together in the Spirit, and it is the Spirit whose action finally binds us together in one fellowship.

To do this we need to distance ourselves in some measure from the conflict itself and from the passions generated by conflict that tend to consume us. When we are obsessed by the conflict, by the hurts done to us, we tend to lose balance and perspective. And the best way to get some distance from the issue is to get closer to God. We need perspective.

Friends will help God give us that perspective. We simply cannot go it alone: loners for Christ are losers. We need people with whom we can share our perplexities, doubts, and struggles. If we go to God alone, we are apt to have our own prejudices confirmed and the battle goes on. Friends tell each other the truth, and often different friends are called upon to meet different crises. Friends frequently can resolve the crisis for us.

In a parish I once served, after I had been there a year I received a letter from a group of parishioners asking me to resign on the grounds of my incompetence as rector, since I was obviously more concerned about social

issues—poverty, racism, the dispossessed—than I was
about the individuals in the parish. When I got the letter,
I was just plain mad. What right did those people have
to write me such a letter? What did they know about me
anyway? All they wanted was not to be reminded of the
ills of our society all around them. What to do? I was so
angry that, fortunately, I didn't know what to do, so I did
nothing except to blow off to my wife—one of the reasons Christian marriage is so important. After a few days
I showed the letter to the senior warden. He said, "Let
me talk to a few people. I'll be back in touch with you."

He soon was. He said he and a few friends had gone
to the writers and talked it over with them, and that I
should forget it. It was, he said, "all taken care of." I
never found out what he meant by that, but the writers,
while they never apologized (which of course they
should have), stayed in the church and as far as I know
lived happily or unhappily ever after. With the passage
of time I came to feel that they were simply missing their
former rector and lashing out in their grief, with me as
the target.

The moral of this little story is: never act in haste,
never in anger, never alone. If you do, you simply agitate the water even more. You become the focus rather
than the Gospel. When the minister becomes the focus,
it's all over. Talk it over with friends and with God. Perhaps they can do what is necessary without you. In time
patience wins out—patience and prayer. Cool it. Pray it.
Learn from it. Move on. Watch. Pray. Work. Preach the
Gospel, not the rights and wrongs of the situation. Pray
to accept the situation as from the hands of God and
then hand it (and yourself) back to God. If God has
called us, he will help us.

If it is God with whom we are dealing, rather than the
situation, what happens to us will be determined more

by God's nature than by ours. Or, to put it another way, our nature will begin to be transformed by his. We shall "put on" Christ; we shall be increasingly informed, remade into his image. It is a matter of "sitting lightly" to the issues that agitate us. This does not mean we no longer care for them: it means we are not excessively attached to them, obsessed by them. To care "passionately" for a thing or a cause or a person is to have our hearts set on that thing or cause or person, but it is to do it in and through God to whom we are most attached, first and last attached. Then, so attached to an everlasting God, he will help us "sit lightly" to anything less than love for them and for us. Our attachments, our obsessions, our addictions, whatever they are—good or bad—are offered to him so we can be free of their control. Then what we want to do is more apt to be what God wants us to do.

Maturity in the Christian faith has to do with learning to deal with conflict, and it also has something to do with decision-making. Let me approach decision-making more directly.

Prayer seems very complicated, and it *is* complicated because faith is complicated, but it is also—like faith—very simple. The language is elementary, using simple words like hello, please, thanks, sorry, help, and goodbye. It is a conversation carried on by two people who trust and love each other. So let us not make it any more difficult or complicated than necessary. Just say, "Mother" or "Father" and then spill out what is in your heart. Kierkegaard once prayed:

Father in heaven!
When the thought of thee wakes in our hearts,
    let it not awaken like a frightened bird
        that flies about in dismay,
but like a child waking from its sleep
    with a heavenly smile.

We often begin by telling God we want: "Please give me this or that." But in time we come to discover that what God wants is to give us himself, so that we want what we want because we love him. He is the one praying with us and through us. Another passage from *The Prayers of Kierkegaard* may help us understand this:

> The immediate person thinks and imagines that when he prays, the important thing he must concentrate on is that God *should hear* what HE is *praying for.* And yet in the true, eternal sense it is just the reverse: the true relation in prayer is not when God hears what is prayed for, but when the *person praying* continues to pray until he is the *one who hears,* who hears what God wills. This immediate person, therefore, uses many words, and, therefore, makes demands in his prayers; the true man of prayer only *attends.*

To attend is to be present. Prayer is being present to God and then responding in accordance with what we believe is God's will. It has to be our decision, not one we try to pass off onto God or somebody else.

A personal illustration about prayer and making decisions. About thirty years ago, I had been dean of the Episcopal Theological School for less than a year when what was then called a calling committee (now called a search committee—interesting change!) from the Diocese of Washington asked me if I would permit my name to be presented for the election of a bishop coadjutor; if elected, I would succeed Bishop Angus Dun when he retired. I said no, I could not do that because I had only just come to the divinity school and had not accomplished what I felt I had to do—in fact, had done nothing.

Nonetheless, when the election was held, I was elected on the first ballot. This was interpreted by some as a sure sign that the Holy Spirit had decided the election. Other friends told me that when a bishop was elected, it represented the voice of the whole church and was therefore more significant than simply serving a parish or a seminary. I was confused. What was God doing? Taking me from Newark to Cambridge, and then within a year apparently changing his mind and sending me to Washington?

So I visited Washington to see the lay of the land and to talk to Bishop Dun, who assured me that when you walked down the aisle escorting the President of the United States from the narthex of the cathedral to his seat in the nave, you really did not have much time to give him your wise counsel on either foreign or domestic policy, so not to worry. I had several interviews with others in the diocese, but they were likewise inconclusive.

On my way back home, I made a detour to talk with Alan Whittemore, a member of the Order of the Holy Cross in West Park, New York, under whose guidance I had gone on several retreats during the fifties. I had telephoned ahead to say that there was some urgency in my seeing him. When he greeted me the next day, he said, "Well, Father, what's the problem?"

I said, "I have just been elected Bishop of Washington."

"Yes?" he replied.

"And," I answered, "I don't know whether to accept or not."

He burst out laughing. "It doesn't make any difference whether you accept or don't accept. All that counts is whether you accept for God's sake or for your own. What do you want to do?"

"I want to decline," I responded.

"Then for God's sake do it," he said. "Do what you want to for your sense of rightness and love of God. Then forget it."

I went on my way with my burden lifted. God was going to get along all right no matter what I did. All I had to do was what I wanted to do and pass it on to God. From my friend I learned a great lesson, probably one of the great ones of my life. God trusted me to make my own decisions for his sake—not unlike Saint Augustine's dictum, "Love God, and do as you like."

Our hearts are not meant to be set on one thing or another—to be bishop or not to be bishop, in this instance—but upon God. If your heart is set upon God and it is your *intent* to focus upon him, to pay attention to him, to try to discern his will for you and discover what he is calling you to be, then things have a way of falling into place.

I tried then, and still try today (without conspicuous success, I must add) to impress this lesson upon men and women who are trying to discern whether they have a call to the ministry. I say, "God doesn't care whether you get ordained or not. All God cares about is whether you are responding to him in your life situation, wherever you find yourself now. If you do this day by day, you will come to a conviction that going into the ministry is what you want to do and you want to do it for God, or it may come to you that this is not what you want to do. All you really have to do is put yourself into God's hands, trust him, and act in accordance with what you want to do right now."

We write the story of our lives chapter by chapter. As we live out the chapter we are in with God, he will lead us into the next one. If we are writing chapter seven, we don't have to worry about chapter nine. That will write itself when the right time comes.

To have one's heart set upon the ordained ministry as an end in itself is to set it up as an idol. We cannot flourish while we are worshiping idols; we flourish only as we worship God. How can we tell? By asking ourselves (or our spouses or trusted friends), "Am I becoming more and more the person I believe God wants me to be—and that I want to be—or less and less?"

Father Whittemore later gave me this helpful bit of advice about decision-making. "You have a decision to make, you have studied all the options, you are clear that any one of them is morally acceptable, but you don't know what to do. Then wait. Put the whole matter in the back of your mind. Let it sit there. Set a date when you will decide. Go to church on that day, make your decision, offer it to God. Then go about it, carrying it out, and no more agonizing!" This way keeps us from taking ourselves too seriously, but it is also responsible decision-making we can live with.

So when you prepare a sermon, give the preparation all the attention and prayer you can. Offer it to the people and to God. And then forget about it. God's Spirit and theirs will do what is best from then on. Then you can go to your Sunday dinner.

What about the place of prayer in a seminary community, or in any community? In the past fifteen or twenty years divinity schools have taken more seriously the task of what is now called "spiritual formation." But this interest in spiritual formation is a recent phenomenon. One or two generations ago scant attention would have been paid to this discipline in most university settings. Even in church seminaries—at least Protestant ones—few courses were offered on the subject, and usually as a subheading called ascetical theology, under historical or systematic theology. It consisted for the most part of a survey of patristic and medieval forms of what was largely monastic piety, and was often assumed to be of interest to a minority of students drawn to "that sort of thing." In any case, ascetical theology existed on the margin of theological education, and I can recall only one course in what was called "Prayer and Personal Devotion" offered at Union Seminary when I was a student.

Today it is quite a different matter. There are now chairs of spirituality, schools of spirituality, workshops on spirituality, retreats and conferences on spirituality, and what can only be termed a veritable flood of books, pamphlets, cassettes, and videotapes on spirituality. If it is true in general that "of making books there is no end, and much study is a weariness of the flesh," it can be even more true of books and studies on spirituality that weary the spirit as well as the flesh!

To study spirituality in a Christian sense is to try to identify and interpret the Spirit of Christ in all human experiences in the Bible, in history, in the church, in other religions, and in other disciplines. Its *practice* is to try to appropriate that Spirit and to live it out in one's own body, community, society, and church. In other words, the end of such study is to have one's own spirit transformed by Christ's Spirit and, therefore, to have a share in transforming one's society.

The spiritual person is one who, to the best of his or her ability, is entering into Christ's Spirit to become more and more wholly Christ's in every aspect of life. For spirituality, the Incarnation means transformation into Christ. Christian spirituality is the opening of oneself to the gift of the Holy Spirit to effect that transformation—both to begin it and to continue in it. It is accomplished by God's grace and our willing participation in that love.

Now how does this understanding of Christian spirituality fit within theological education? How does spirituality face theological education—as friend or enemy? Does theological education encompass spirituality or does spirituality encompass theological education? Or do they just not mix, like oil and water, and so can never belong together?

A friend of mine who is a highly respected theological educator has said, "There should be no place in a seminary for spirituality. A seminary is a place to learn how to think theologically, to understand the scriptures, to learn how the people of God have tried to live the Gospel generation after generation. It is essentially a rigorous academic enterprise. To introduce spirituality is to introduce confusion." And (he probably meant) softheadedness.

In contrast to this, students in seminary will often say, "In the midst of all the academic responsibilities and all the theological discussions, I hope to be able to maintain and strengthen my personal relationship to Jesus Christ. I hope to enrich my prayer life and use the classes and assignments, as well as my personal prayers, to refresh my faith." This, I believe, states the issue and the challenge very clearly.

Christian prayer means taking seriously the intellectual and academic disciplines offered in a theological seminary and participating in the rigors of study with a willing spirit. Some forms of spirituality seem to me to be mindless, ones with an exclusive emphasis upon the conversion of the heart while ignoring the mind. A divinity school provides a place for an honest, open, rigorous search for the meaning of the human enterprise. The *acesis* or discipline of spirituality in a seminary community is best expressed in doing the assignments, getting the papers in on time, and enduring the judgment of examination and grades.

Spirituality is not meant, therefore, to be set over against biblical, theological, historical, and pastoral studies, but to include them, participate in them, honor them. To go deeply into the intellectual and academic enterprise is to go deeply into one side of Christian devotion.

There is, of course, the other side of Christian devotion, a complementary side. While the *study* of spirituality and the disciplines of theological education are important, what is also sought for, as the quotation from the student makes clear, is the *experience* of spirituality. Just how does one experience God, know Christ personally, live in the Holy Spirit? What are the means, beyond reason, that exist in a seminary community to help us know "Christ and him crucified" and to make possible our transformation into Christ—or, more accurately, to begin that transformation?

What is given is the community: men and women living together in personal relationships, bound together in the common enterprise of theological education by a spirit which at its best is the Holy Spirit. This caring community lives not by reason but by faith. Christian spirituality in theological education means a faith community sustained by personal relationships motivated by mutual concern for the well-being of others; a concern for issues of peace and justice so that the mind of Christ might be perceived. The spirituality of any particular seminary rises from the spirituality of those who make it up: those who teach and those who learn and, perhaps especially, those who in their learning do the teaching. We are called to share with one another what we know of "the deep things of God."

We are called, then, in any community to love God with all our heart, soul, and mind, and our neighbors as ourselves. And just as theological education includes theological studies, so it includes putting up with each others' idiosyncrasies, prejudices, and even apparent bad spirit at times. It means praying for one another. A little humility, a little gentleness, a little of not getting one's own way, all play their part in helping spirituality develop within oneself and within one's community. While in theory "spirituality" is a big, all-encompassing word, in practice it simply means trusting God, having faith in God when he is hidden; paying attention to God in prayer and worship; and not making too much of oneself, before either God or one's neighbor. This is the spirit that rises out of a community of Christian persons.

Spiritual formation is largely developed, learned, and taught by the community's life. The teacher of spirituality can point throughout history to those who have caught that spirit over generations and shown it in their lives, can help individuals in their own spiritual growth, and can simply be a presence in the community.

In my experience, a teacher of spirituality can do three things. First, he or she can introduce students to the great classics of Christian devotion. A "learned ministry" assumes that one knows the literature of the church, both East and West, and has appropriated a first-hand knowledge of some of the great Christian classics.

Second, a teacher can share his or her own insights into the spiritual life. I do not think this can often be done in formal lectures, but is better offered in informal discussion with no more than fifteen students, so there can be easy give and take. In this setting it is possible to present aspects of prayer from the simplest to the most "mystical" heights in an orderly fashion.

Finally, a teacher can help to create an atmosphere in which students share their own spiritual quests, convictions, and contributions. In this field, probably more than any other discipline, the students teach each other. Being able to do this naturally, freely, and without embarrassment is important preparation for preaching, where personal witness is essential if the sermon is to have integrity and to be useful to others. I have listened to student meditations on trees, dancing, swimming, breathing, dreaming, Bible stories, serving at soup kitchens, sexuality, Jesus as Lover, and the Holy Eucharist—and have been edified by each one. This is one area of theological education where students can make their own contributions to each other as active teachers who give rather than, as so often happens, passive students who simply take everything in—or don't.

In the community of those preparing for ministry, the spirit is also nurtured by common worship. The simple singing of hymns, the offering of prayers, the blessing of bread and wine are all part of spiritual formation. A regular rhythm of praise and intercession, confession and thanksgiving is an integral part of community life that provides the necessary balance to personal piety, which by itself can become arid, dry up, and disappear, or can sow the seeds of self-righteousness whereby we are tempted to thank God we are not as others are. John Donne in one sermon said:

> I believe in the Holy Ghost, but doe not finde him, if I seeke him only in private prayer; But in Ecclesia, when I goe to meet him in the Church, when I seeke him where hee hath promised to be found...in his Ordinances, and meanes of salvation in his Church, instantly the savour of this Myrre is exalted and multiplied upon me.

Participation in community worship as well as private prayer together form the inner life in Christ, which finally prepares the preacher to preach. This is the church where the Word is preached and the sacraments administered. This is the church that nourishes the preacher throughout his or her ministry. The place to begin is where the preacher begins, right here in this community, this branch of Christ's church.

At the beginning of the first chapter, I stated my conviction that prayer and preaching are bound together because of the call by God to the preacher to preach. This is to possess something of the conviction Jeremiah had that God had formed him in the womb, knew him before he was born, and created him to preach. The response to that call, both in preaching and in living, is the preacher's prayer. Keeping alive the sense that one is preaching because God has called one to preach is a by-product of prayer, and probably more than any other factor sustains the preacher during the dry places and periods that seem inevitably to arise during a life of ministry. That is the preacher's vocation.

How to keep that sense of vocation? It will come as no surprise to you if I say that, first of all, one needs time and one needs silence. No one in the parish ministry is given much time. Instead, people want your time, keep taking it away from you. So you have to be firm in taking time for yourself—for yourself and God.

What do you do with that time with God? Well, first of all, nothing. Just be content to sit or walk. There is a wonderful phrase, *solvitur ambulandon:* things get sorted out and fall into place as you amble along. "Consider the lilies of the field," our Lord counsels us. Don't plant them. Don't pluck them. Don't eat them. Just look at them.

Then you can marvel at God and his ways. See what wonders he performs, like letting the sun rise and letting it sink, day in, day out, forever. Like people living and loving, being born, counting for something, growing old, dying—rejoicing, trusting, laughing, waiting.

Second, take time to read and study and pray. I put them together because they belong together, as our mind feeds our spirit and comes to lodge in our heart. You cannot put something out if nothing is coming in. All the words written over the ages provide us with the thinking and experiences of others so we may have some substance in our system as we ponder the Word.

Third (though it could just as well come first, for there are no priorities among these ways of spending time, they belong all together), take time with your family, with special friends who take you just as you are and are glad you are just as you are. Family and friends provide us with natural support groups. They are given by God; we are meant to enjoy them and they us. Take time to have fun. That apocryphal saying, "All work and no play makes Jack a dull boy," is Gospel truth.

I could go on giving good advice indefinitely, and probably you would pay no more attention to it than my students have, or than I have paid to my teachers. More than advice, we need people around us who care for us, who are committed to their own vocation, and who take God seriously as the giver of their lives. Generally speaking, if we hang around people like that, after a while we catch on—unless, of course, we don't. Advice is, in my experience, of limited value both in the giving and receiving.

All we can do, finally, is not to be disobedient to whatever heavenly vision has been given us and to continue to learn from the Lord who is high and lifted up. It is from that vision we preach; it is that vision given to our people that will help them see their vision. And if we do that, then the sermons we preach will be God's Word for his people.

Preaching is, in fact, a wonderful, rich, at times difficult, but always grace-filled vocation. Take your time. Don't ever be afraid, and don't ever give up. Be the best person you can be. Your best sermons will be you at your best, and you at your best will be your best sermons.